ISEE
LOWER LEVEL
PRACTICE TESTS

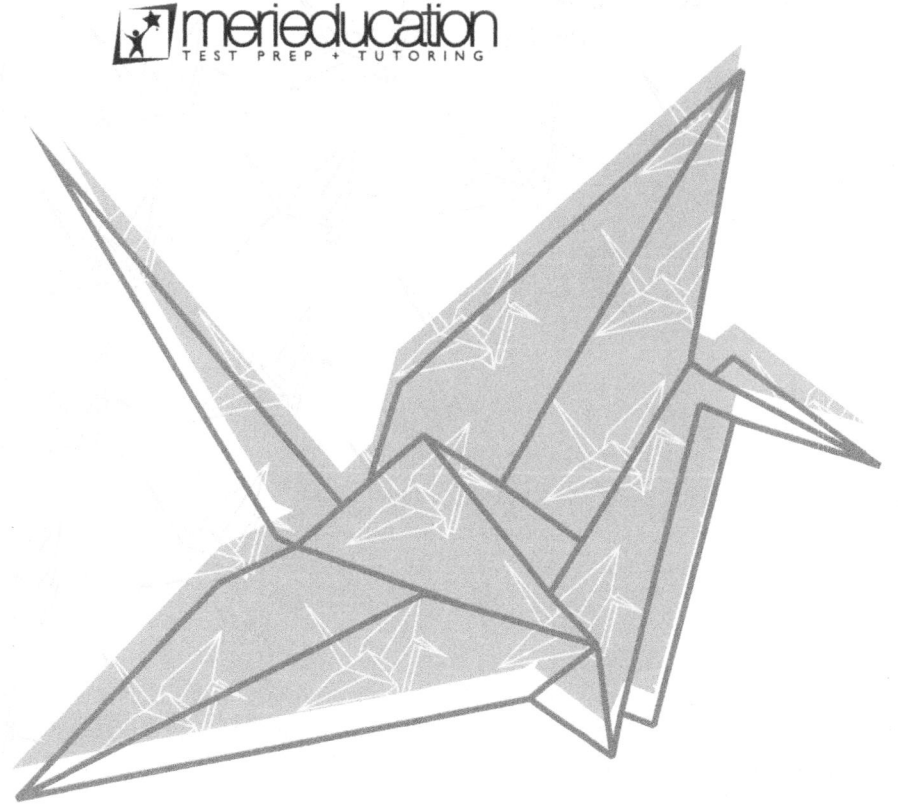

merieducation
TEST PREP + TUTORING

NAME: _____

TABLE OF CONTENTS

TEST #1: Meri-ISEE LL1 5
    Verbal Reasoning 6
    Quantitative Reasoning 12
    Reading Comprehension 18
    Mathematics Achievement 28
    Essay 37

TEST #2: Meri-ISEE LL2 39
    Verbal Reasoning 40
    Quantitative Reasoning 46
    Reading Comprehension 54
    Mathematics Achievement 64
    Essay 71

TEST #3: Meri-ISEE LL3 73
    Verbal Reasoning 74
    Quantitative Reasoning 80
    Reading Comprehension 88
    Mathematics Achievement 98
    Essay 107

TEST #4: Meri-ISEE LL4 109
    Verbal Reasoning 110
    Quantitative Reasoning 116
    Reading Comprehension 124
    Mathematics Achievement 134
    Essay 141

TEST #5: Meri-ISEE LL5 143
    Verbal Reasoning 144
    Quantitative Reasoning 150
    Reading Comprehension 158
    Mathematics Achievement 168
    Essay 175

TEST ANSWER KEYS 177

Section 1: Verbal Reasoning
34 Questions — 20 Minutes
Part One — Synonyms

Directions: Select the word that is most nearly the same in meaning as the word in capital letters.

---

1. HECTIC:

    (A) ardent
    (B) frenetic
    (C) full
    (D) peaceful

2. VANQUISH:

    (A) aid
    (B) blister
    (C) disprove
    (D) overthrow

3. MANIPULATE:

    (A) control
    (B) freedom
    (C) help
    (D) necessary

4. MARVEL:

    (A) amazed
    (B) bored
    (C) helpful
    (D) ignorant

5. DEPLETE:

    (A) develop
    (B) diminish
    (C) follow
    (D) force

6. COMPENSATE:

    (A) abolish
    (B) destroy
    (C) refund
    (D) slow

7. CONFINE:

    (A) avoid
    (B) destroy
    (C) detain
    (D) liberate

8. TONE:

    (A) action
    (B) carriage
    (C) inflection
    (D) management

Go on to the next page.

VR   1

9. CONQUER:

   (A) defeat
   (B) give
   (C) help
   (D) take

10. DEFY:

    (A) assist
    (B) beard
    (C) resist
    (D) summon

11. ORIGINAL:

    (A) authentic
    (B) deceitful
    (C) helpful
    (D) necessary

12. NOURISHING:

    (A) clear
    (B) healthful
    (C) willful
    (D) wishful

13. ATTENTIVE:

    (A) aware
    (B) negligent
    (C) strange
    (D) wise

14. CALCULATE:

    (A) determine
    (B) estimate
    (C) trade
    (D) unravel

15. RESTORE:

    (A) decline
    (B) help
    (C) purge
    (D) repair

16. CURIOUSLY:

    (A) nicely
    (B) normally
    (C) quietly
    (D) specially

17. PUZZLING:

    (A) clear
    (B) confusing
    (C) occult
    (D) snarled

Go on to the next page. ➤

VR

Part Two — Sentence Completion

Directions: Select the word that best completes the sentence.

18. We did not know if it was possible to ------- our mistake, but we were going to try to make sure nobody found out.

    (A) conceal
    (B) humor
    (C) liberate
    (D) prevent

19. How did she ------- the wrong answers? She couldn't have known which were right and wrong.

    (A) control
    (B) eliminate
    (C) magnify
    (D) pacify

20. There are many ------- when working with chemicals; you have to make sure to wear goggles and safety equipment.

    (A) areas
    (B) hazards
    (C) tragedies
    (D) unknown

21. We couldn't believe when our teacher ------- us, telling us that we would not pass the class if we did not clean his car.

    (A) exposed
    (B) helped
    (C) knew
    (D) threatened

22. Delilah grew up in the -------, spending her days taking care of the farm and exploring the fields and forests.

    (A) city
    (B) countryside
    (C) sewer
    (D) United States

23. Jimmy knew that his mom had complete ------- of the TV, for he could never choose what he wanted to watch.

    (A) control
    (B) help
    (C) magnification
    (D) speeches

Go on to the next page. ➤

VR

24. Her brothers were proving to be ------- to the plan; she couldn't even get past the gate without them messing up and alerting the guards.

    (A) detrimental
    (B) farcical
    (C) helpful
    (D) kind

25. Evan knew that playing with his friends was -------, for he would eventually have to go home.

    (A) forever
    (B) primary
    (C) sentimental
    (D) temporary

26. Food was ------- for the owl family; they had to search for many days before finding a meal.

    (A) encompassing
    (B) healthy
    (C) plentiful
    (D) scarce

27. The rebels decided to overthrow the -------, which had oppressed them their entire lives.

    (A) concrete
    (B) government
    (C) restaurants
    (D) schools

28. Evie decided that the best way to prove her ------- to Eric was by getting a tattoo of him, which ended up only pushing Eric further away.

    (A) devotion
    (B) fullness
    (C) happenstance
    (D) hatred

29. One of the most ------- food allergies is being allergic to peanuts.

    (A) common
    (B) destructive
    (C) helpful
    (D) rare

30. John wanted to go to as many travel ------- as possible while on vacation.

    (A) businesses
    (B) destinations
    (C) homes
    (D) operations

31. The adventurers set out on their first -------, a daring adventure into the forest.

    (A) commute
    (B) problem
    (C) vacation
    (D) voyage

Go on to the next page.

VR

32. The man used bug spray as a(n) ------- to make sure that he wasn't bitten by mosquitoes.

    (A) attractor
    (B) device
    (C) noise
    (D) repellant

33. Janet had the ------- of a child; she was constantly dreaming up new worlds and quirky characters for her books.

    (A) humor
    (B) imagination
    (C) intelligence
    (D) patience

34. Alan did not know how to ------- the problem; he had tried everything to stop it from happening.

    (A) analyze
    (B) cause
    (C) have
    (D) prevent

QR 2

Section 2: Quantitative Reasoning
38 Questions — 35 Minutes

---

1. Charles is thinking of a whole number greater than 5 and less than 9. Ted starts to guess, and Charles says the number is also greater than 7 and less than 12. What number is Charles thinking of?

   (A) 5
   (B) 6
   (C) 7
   (D) 8

2. Use the information below to answer the question.

   $$10 + \blacksquare = 17$$
   $$10 - \bullet = 7$$

   What is $\blacksquare \times \bullet$ equal to?

   (A) 0
   (B) 10
   (C) 21
   (D) 119

3. Which of these fractions is the smallest?

   (A) $\frac{3}{8}$
   (B) $\frac{5}{16}$
   (C) $\frac{1}{2}$
   (D) $\frac{7}{8}$

4. If the perimeter of an equilateral triangle is $24y$, what is the length of one side?

   (A) 6
   (B) 8
   (C) $6y$
   (D) $8y$

5. Which of the following has exactly 6 lines of symmetry?

   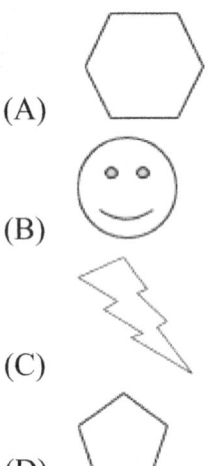

   (A)
   (B)
   (C)
   (D)

6. David and his 3 friends found 100 diamonds one day, and decided to share them equally. Which of the following equations best fits the situation?

   (A) $100 \times 4 = 400$
   (B) $100 \div 4 = 25$
   (C) $100 \times 3 = 300$
   (D) $100 \div 3 = 33$

Go on to the next page. ➤

QR 2

7. Which of the following is divisible by 3?

   (A) 724
   (B) 725
   (C) 726
   (D) 727

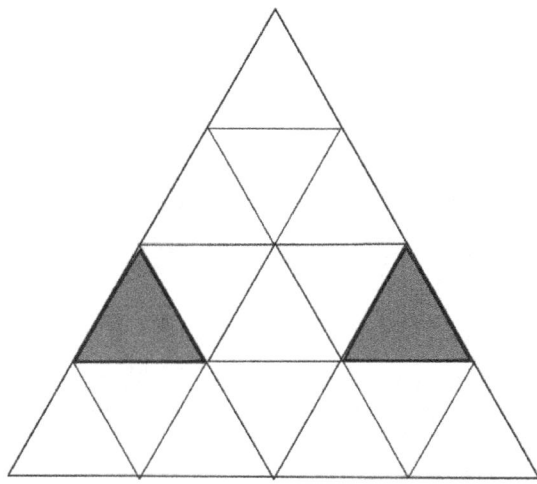

8. What fraction of the above triangle is not shaded?

   (A) $\frac{1}{8}$
   (B) $\frac{2}{16}$
   (C) $\frac{2}{9}$
   (D) $\frac{7}{8}$

9. Which of the following correctly shows the commutative property?

   (A) $\Delta + \Pi = \Delta\Pi$
   (B) $\Delta + \Pi = \Pi + \Delta$
   (C) $\Theta(\Delta + \Pi) = \Theta\Delta + \Theta\Pi$
   (D) $(\Delta + \Pi) + \Theta = \Delta + (\Pi + \Theta)$

10. Joseph and Kim are riding their bikes at the same speed. It takes Joseph takes 12 minutes to ride 5 miles. At this rate, how long will it take Kim to ride 20 miles?

    (A) 12 minutes
    (B) 20 minutes
    (C) 36 minutes
    (D) 48 minutes

11. In a bag of 20 marbles, 4 are green, 3 are red, and the rest are blue. If a marble is taken from the bag at random, what is the probability of selecting a blue marble?

    (A) $\frac{1}{20}$
    (B) $\frac{1}{3}$
    (C) $\frac{7}{20}$
    (D) $\frac{13}{20}$

12. Which of the following is a possible value for x?

    $$2x + 5 = 17$$

    (A) 6
    (B) 7
    (C) 8
    (D) 9

Go on to the next page. ➤

QR

13. A customer at a store buys the following items: 6 apples which are $0.99 for three, 2 milk gallons which are $2.97 each, and 1 loaf of bread which is $1.99. Estimate the total cost of these groceries.

    (A) $14
    (B) $10
    (C) $8
    (D) $6

14. In the 5th grade class, 18% of students prefer vanilla ice cream. 37% prefer chocolate, and 20% prefer strawberry, and the rest prefer a different flavor. What percent of students prefer a different flavor?

    (A) 15%
    (B) 25%
    (C) 35%
    (D) 40%

15. The product $3 \times 5 \times 4 \times 8$ is equal to the product of 12 and which of the following?

    (A) 15
    (B) 20
    (C) 24
    (D) 40

16. In a jumbo bag of lollipops, there are an equal amount of raspberry, watermelon, cherry, and green apple pops. Which of the following could be the total number of lollipops in a jumbo bag?

    (A) 39
    (B) 42
    (C) 48
    (D) 62

17. Which of the following is the largest integer smaller than 14.998?

    (A) 14
    (B) 15
    (C) 16
    (D) 17

18. In baseball, you must run around a square with side lengths of 90 feet. If Jeff runs all the way around the bases, how many feet did he run?

    (A) 180 feet
    (B) 270 feet
    (C) 360 feet
    (D) 450 feet

19. Which of the following is NOT equal to 25% ?

    (A) $\frac{1}{8}$
    (B) $\frac{1}{4}$
    (C) .25
    (D) $.15 + .05 \times 2$

Go on to the next page. ➤

QR 2

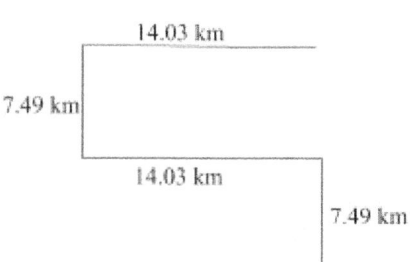

20. What is the approximate length of the road pictured above?

    (A) 42 km
    (B) 43 km
    (C) 44 km
    (D) 45 km

21. Which of the following units is most appropriate to use when measuring the height of a building?

    (A) tons
    (B) hertz
    (C) kilometers
    (D) meters

22. A rectangular canvas is 18 inches by 12 inches. What is the perimeter of this canvas?

    (A) 40 inches
    (B) 60 inches
    (C) 108 inches
    (D) 216 inches

23. Sean and Priscilla are riding in their canoes at the same speed. If Sean can get from his cabin to Viper Rock which is 4 miles downstream in 10 minutes, how long will it take Priscilla to reach Python Point which is 10 miles downstream?

    (A) 15 minutes
    (B) 20 minutes
    (C) 25 minutes
    (D) 30 minutes

24. A salesman makes 20% commission on all sales of electronics. If he sold $400 on electronics and $100 on toy sales, how much commission does the salesman make?

    (A) $20
    (B) $80
    (C) $100
    (D) $120

25. Gina is twice as old as four years less than her younger sister's age. If her younger sister is thirteen, how old is Gina?

    (A) 18 years old
    (B) 20 years old
    (C) 22 years old
    (D) 24 years old

Go on to the next page. ➤

QR

26. Which of the following numbers comes next in the sequence below?

    3, 6, 12, 24, . . .

    (A) 27
    (B) 38
    (C) 48
    (D) 60

27. The weights of 4 cats are 12.325, 12.320, 11.987, and 12.235 pounds. Which of the following shows the weights in order from largest to smallest?

    (A) 12.325, 12.320, 12.235, 11.987
    (B) 11.987, 12.235, 12.320, 12.325
    (C) 12.325, 12.235, 12.320, 11.987
    (D) 11.987, 12.325, 12.320, 12.235

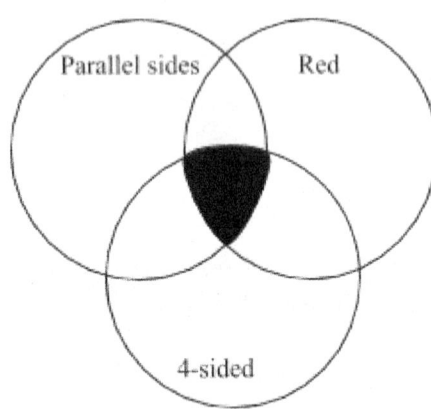

28. Which of the following would be in the section shaded above?

    (A) a blue square
    (B) a red trapezoid
    (C) a red triangle
    (D) a red rhombus

29. Last season, there were 80 games at home. Vince went to 60 of these games. What percent of the games did Vince miss?

    (A) 20 percent
    (B) 25 percent
    (C) 60 percent
    (D) 75 percent

30. Nicole earns $25 from doing chores around the house for the week. She spends $10.43 on a movie ticket and $7.68 on food. How much does Nicole have left over?

    (A) $5.89
    (B) $6.89
    (C) $18.11
    (D) $19.11

31. All of the 23 students in the speech class have to make a 5 minute speech on their favorite historical figure. How long will presentations last?

    (A) 1 hour 45 minutes
    (B) 1 hour 50 minutes
    (C) 1 hour 55 minutes
    (D) 2 hours 5 minutes

32. 23 is what percent of 46?

    (A) 23 percent
    (B) 25 percent
    (C) 45 percent
    (D) 50 percent

Go on to the next page. ➤

QR 2

33. Three eighths of the students in a class has a dog. If 12 students have a dog, how many total students are there in the class?

    (A) 12
    (B) 20
    (C) 24
    (D) 32

34. Which of the following is worth the most?

    (A) 2 quarters and a dime
    (B) 2 quarters and 2 nickels
    (C) 7 dimes
    (D) 18 nickels

35. If $x + 7 = 12$, and $2 - y = 3$, what is $x + y$?

    (A) -1
    (B) 5
    (C) 4
    (D) 6

36. In a group of 36 people, ⅔ live in the city. How many people live in the suburbs?

    (A) 12
    (B) 24
    (C) 30
    (D) Cannot be determined

37. Which of the following is the best estimate of the product of 201 and 49.95.

    (A) 10,000
    (B) 2,000
    (C) 1,500
    (D) 1,000

38. Roosevelt high school's star runner beat the previous 400 meter dash record of 50.27 seconds by a second and a half. What is the new record?

    (A) 48.77 seconds
    (B) 49 seconds
    (C) 51.27 seconds
    (D) 51.77 seconds

STOP.

RC 3

Section 3: Reading Comprehension
25 Questions — 25 Minutes

Questions 1-5

1   For decades, when anyone thought about
2 printing something from a computer, he or
3 she might have expected words or images
4 produced in black or maybe even color ink
5 on sheets of paper. However, printing from
6 computers is not just about flat text or
7 pictures on paper anymore.
8   3D printers make three-dimensional,
9 solid objects from digital files. To make a 3D
10 print, a person starts by creating a 3D image
11 on a computer, usually using a CAD
12 (Computer Aided Design) file. In order to
13 create a 3D model on a computer, one can
14 use 3D modeling software or a 3D scanner
15 to create a digital copy of an object.
16   In order to prepare a 3D model for
17 printing, it goes through a process called
18 slicing. Slicing is dividing the 3D model
19 into multiple horizontal layers so that it
20 can be printed layer by layer.
21   There are many ways that a 3D printer
22 produces its prints. One of the most common
23 ways is to generate one layer at a time using
24 powders made of resin or plastic. Another
25 way is to melt or soften materials together.
26 Still another way is to spray the layers until
27 the model is completely built up.

28   There are many industries now that
29 use 3D printing to create their products.
30 Manufacturers make complete products or
31 parts, medical companies make surgical
32 instruments for patients, fashion designers
33 make clothes, and gourmet chefs even make
34 fancy-looking desserts and dishes.
35   These days, students who attend schools
36 of all levels may have access to 3D printers.
37 Those who support having 3D printers as
38 part of school lessons say that this new
39 technology is great for STEM education,
40 art class creations, visual and touch-based
41 learners, and building a sense of community
42 for students as they work on 3D projects
43 together.
44   Then, are 3D printers worth it? Well,
45 even though there are more affordable
46 models for under $500, industrial-grade 3D
47 printers can be priced anywhere from
48 $5,000-$500,000. The choice is up to
49 the individual consumer. Some questions to
50 ask include "what would I make with it?"
51 or "how often will I use it?" At any rate, it
52 seems that 3D printing is becoming more
53 and more a part of our advancing world.

Go on to the next page. ➤

RC   3

1. The primary purpose of this passage is to

    (A) analyze how important 3D printers are for society.
    (B) discuss what kind of schools might benefit from 3D printing.
    (C) describe how 3D printers work and what they can do.
    (D) state the definition of 3D printing in a scientific way.

2. The function of the fourth paragraph (lines 21-27) is to

    (A) summarize the entire passage.
    (B) provide examples that support the author's argument.
    (C) describe the different types of printers that people use.
    (D) describe the different ways that 3D printers make prints.

3. The author's attitude toward 3D printing is best described as

    (A) confused.
    (B) doubtful.
    (C) optimistic.
    (D) surprised.

4. In line 46, "industrial-grade" most nearly means

    (A) cellular.
    (B) luxurious.
    (C) professional-level.
    (D) shabby.

5. What can be inferred from the last sentence (lines 51-53)?

    (A) 3D printers are significant for artificial intelligence.
    (B) The author believes that everyone should own a 3D printer.
    (C) 3D printers are too expensive.
    (D) People will be seeing a lot more 3D printers in the future.

Go on to the next page. ➤

RC

Questions 6-10

One summer, I went on an 18-mile hike through some lush green mountains in the Poconos of New York. There were several other teenagers in my group. We all had on large backpacks filled with various items for our day-long journey through the wilderness. My backpack had a rain poncho in it, along with a large bottle of water, a huge bag of trail mix, some sunscreen, and a thin emergency blanket.

There were no treacherous events or wild beast encounters along the way. The only thing that really happened to me was great exhaustion. I was not used to such enormous treks in my life—physically or mentally.

I was so tired that I trailed behind everyone almost the entire time. I wasn't surprised; I usually finished near-to-last or last during mile-runs or races in gym class. I just knew that I was neither a runner nor a walker, nor a hiker for that matter.

I decided to go on this trip mostly because a lot of my friends were going. However, as luck would have it, none of my good friends ended up in my hiking group. All the others who had left me behind had little reason to wait up for me.

Too exhausted to feel alone, I happily filled the long gaps of grassy plants between my group and me with loud complaints of how tired I was, how unappetizing trail mix was, and how I longed to just lie down and sleep.

A few miles from the end, a boy ran all the way from the front to stroll by my side. I felt I had to stop complaining with him around, so I asked him why he decided to stay with me when I was so slow. He didn't say much in reply, but he joined in on my complaints. The whole way back to the cabins, I wondered if he walked with me because he was really weary, or if keeping pace with me actually drained him more.

RC

6. Which statement best expresses the main idea of the passage?

   (A) The narrator has a difficult time and does not appreciate a nature hike.
   (B) Teenagers get tired too easily and should rest more.
   (C) The Poconos are lush and green in the summer.
   (D) It is important to take the right equipment on a hike.

7. The word "treacherous" in line 11 most nearly means

   (A) dangerous
   (B) educational
   (C) shiny
   (D) skillful

8. According to the passage, how did the narrator react when the boy came to walk alongside her?

   (A) The narrator got very upset and asked him a lot of questions.
   (B) The narrator became happy and got a warm feeling inside.
   (C) The narrator felt a burst of energy and bolted to the front of the group.
   (D) The narrator questioned the boy's motives.

9. Which word best characterizes the attitude of the narrator?

   (A) cheerful
   (B) contented
   (C) nervous
   (D) unappreciative

10. What is the function of the fifth paragraph (lines 29-34)?

    (A) It describes the visual beauty of the hike.
    (B) It shows that the narrator is starting to express inner frustrations out loud.
    (C) It establishes the deep loneliness of the narrator.
    (D) It lists the narrator's favorite hobbies.

Go on to the next page. ➤

Questions 11-15

Near the border of Connecticut on the southern tip of New York state is a hamlet in the town of Kent. It is called Ludingtonville, named after a settler named Henry Ludington. He was a rich landowner and a commander of a volunteer regiment during the American Revolutionary War. Though he was famous in his own right, another Ludington family member also deserves much acclaim: his daughter, Sybil.

Perhaps not many people know who Sybil Ludington is because her recognition is eclipsed by that of Paul Revere. However, she performed a ride similar to that of Revere's, despite being the only woman and merely 16 years old.

In April of 1777, Ludington rode her horse, Star, 40 miles to warn hundreds of militiamen that British troops were about to attack Danbury, Connecticut. Danbury was a target because American army supplies were stored there. She got involved in the war in order to help her father and his troops.

Courageously, the teenaged Sybil started her journey alone, well after sunset in long stretches of darkness. She used a stick to prod her horse, knock on doors, and even fend off a robber on the road.

As a result of Ludington's undertaking, there were fewer American casualties during the British attack on Danbury. In addition, the Americans were able to drive out their enemy at the start of the next battle.

Although Sybil Ludington is not as well-known today, her efforts did not go unnoticed in her time. General Washington gave personal thanks to Sybil, and her father Henry received written congratulations from Alexander Hamilton for what happened at Danbury.

Today, there stands a statue of Sybil Ludington in Carmel, New York. The art piece, sculpted by Anna Hyatt Huntington, was unveiled in 1935. In it, Ludington is on her horse, gripping the reins with one hand while raising a sturdy stick with the other.

RC   3

11. The main idea of this passage is to

    (A) discuss the history of Ludingtonville.
    (B) prove that Sybil Ludington helped save the British troops.
    (C) bring light to the feats of Sybil Ludington.
    (D) show that Sybil Ludington rode with Paul Revere on his Midnight Ride.

12. What is the purpose of the first paragraph (lines 1-10)?

    (A) It shows the importance of Ludingtonville and Kent.
    (B) It provides background for the story of Sybil Ludington.
    (C) It sets the scene for the night of Sybil Ludington's ride.
    (D) It sets up the accomplishments of Henry Ludington.

13. In line 13, "eclipsed" most nearly means

    (A) destroyed.
    (B) helped.
    (C) mixed.
    (D) overshadowed.

14. The author's attitude toward Sybil Ludington is best described as

    (A) admiring.
    (B) hostile.
    (C) indirect.
    (D) mocking.

15. According to the passage, how did Sybil Ludington's ride contribute to war efforts?

    (A) She provided help to Paul Revere by riding 40 miles with him.
    (B) She was exceptionally talented at taking care of horses.
    (C) She fought British troops on horseback with a stick.
    (D) She warned American militiamen of an attack on Danbury.

Go on to the next page. ➤

Questions 16-20

In an early version of the story of Aladdin in *The Book of One Thousand and One Tales*, there are actually two genies. One of them comes from a ring that Aladdin wears, and another one comes from the famous magic lamp.

Aladdin starts out as a very poor thief who lives somewhere in China when a sorcerer recruits him by setting him up as a wealthy merchant. However, the sorcerer has ulterior motives. He wants to use Aladdin for his superior stealing skills. The sorcerer knows about the powers of the magic lamp, which is hidden in a cave full of obstacles. He gives Aladdin his own magic ring to help retrieve the treasured item.

Aladdin first uses the magic ring when he finds himself trapped in the tricky cave. He wrings his hands in nervousness, thus rubbing the ring as well. Suddenly, a genie appears and helps Aladdin escape from the cave.

The more powerful genie appears when the magic lamp, now in Aladdin's possession, gets cleaned. This famed genie makes Aladdin rich, powerful, and eligible to marry the sultan's daughter.

Aladdin's new position seems to rid him of the need for the less powerful genie of the magic ring. However, the deceitful sorcerer returns and manages to acquire everything that Aladdin had by stealing the magic lamp. As a result, Aladdin summons the first genie again, using the magic ring. Though this genie cannot overcome the work of the genie from the magic lamp, he can get Aladdin to where he needs to be to eventually defeat the sorcerer.

Later versions of the Aladdin story eliminate the first genie because he cannot grant Aladdin lavish riches. However, he is able to get Aladdin out of significant trouble in his own ways. Perhaps we can all learn that sometimes necessary help comes from from humble or forgotten places.

RC

3

16. The primary purpose of the passage is to

    (A) prove that there are various versions of Aladdin that originate from prehistoric times.
    (B) convey that there was a little-known additional character in the story of Aladdin.
    (C) give a contemporary rendition of the story of Aladdin.
    (D) provide a detailed profile of the evil sorcerer

17. In the opening sentence of the passage (lines 1-3), it is implied that

    (A) there are different versions of Aladdin from different times.
    (B) *The Book* of *One Thousand and One Tales* was written recently.
    (C) most people knew about the two genies.
    (D) nobody knows the story of Aladdin.

18. In line 11, the word "ulterior" most nearly means

    (A) open.
    (B) regular.
    (C) secret.
    (D) single.

19. In the second paragraph (lines 7-17), the author implies that Aladdin is

    (A) an experienced and successful merchant.
    (B) happy with his current situation.
    (C) initially suspicious of the sorcerer.
    (D) trusting of the sorcerer.

20. According to the passage, what is the significance of the genie from the magic ring?

    (A) The genie from the magic ring proved to be much more powerful than the genie from the magic lamp.
    (B) The genie from the magic ring proved to be insignificant after all.
    (C) The genie from the magic lamp was not the only genie that Aladdin needed.
    (D) The genie from the magic ring was equally as powerful as the genie from the magic lamp.

Go on to the next page. ➤

Questions 21-25

Depicted on the official flag of the state of California is a large brown bear that is modeled after the last California grizzly bear in captivity. Consequently, California's state flag is often called the bear flag. Unfortunately, there are no more California grizzly bears in California or anywhere else because they are now extinct.

The California grizzly was a subspecies of the grizzly bear, or the North American brown bear. Although the California grizzly is the most genetically similar to the North American grizzly, in size and coloring, it looked more like the grizzlies that are found near the southern coast of Alaska, called Kodiak bears. California grizzlies were known for their imposing size, stunning beauty, and tremendous strength.

Sadly, California grizzlies were targeted in the early 1800s because, at that time, New Spain was establishing ranchos and raising livestock. The native bears attacked the herds, and thus became regular hunting targets of the ranchers. The bears were also captured—California grizzlies were pitted against fighting bulls for public entertainment.

When gold was discovered in California in 1848, the population surge spelled more trouble for the bears. By the early 1900s, almost every California grizzly was hunted and killed.

The last California grizzly in captivity died in 1911 and is now preserved at the California Academy of Sciences in San Francisco. Its name was "Monarch."

RC   3

21. The passage is primarily concerned with describing

    (A) the origin of the state of California.
    (B) the California grizzly and the story of its extinction.
    (C) the history of bullfighting in California.
    (D) the story of Monarch's capture.

22. The passage answers which of these following questions?

    (A) What are the colors of the official state flag of California?
    (B) Where was the last California grizzly seen in nature?
    (C) What other animals native to California are extinct?
    (D) Where are Kodiak bears found?

23. It can be inferred from the fourth paragraph (lines 28-32) that

    (A) in 1848, California grizzlies began to die of natural causes.
    (B) the bears became more aggressive when people discovered gold in California.
    (C) more people coming to California meant more hunters.
    (D) California gold was toxic to California grizzlies.

24. In line 29, "surge" most nearly means

    (A) decrease.
    (B) growth.
    (C) master.
    (D) purge.

25. The author's attitude toward the extinction of California grizzlies is best described as

    (A) detached.
    (B) discontent.
    (C) hopeful.
    (D) overpowering.

STOP.

MA 4

Section 4: Mathematics Achievement
30 Questions — 30 Minutes

---

1. Use the rectangle to answer the question.

   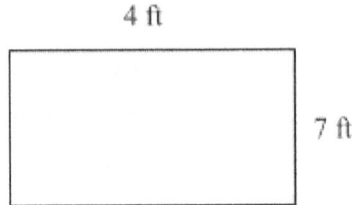

   What is the perimeter of the rectangle?
   ($P = 2L + 2W$)

   (A) 11 feet
   (B) 22 feet
   (C) 28 feet
   (D) 121 feet

2. A total of 37 children were asked which type of pet (dog, cat, or fish) was their favorite. If 21 preferred dogs, and 9 preferred cats, how many children preferred fish?

   (A) 5
   (B) 7
   (C) 9
   (D) 11

3. What type of triangle has sides that are all equal in length?

   (A) isosceles
   (B) obtuse
   (C) acute
   (D) equilateral

4. What is the standard form for three hundred twenty-six thousand fifty-three?

   (A) 326,530
   (B) 302,653
   (C) 326,053
   (D) 326,503

5. Use the number line to answer the question.

   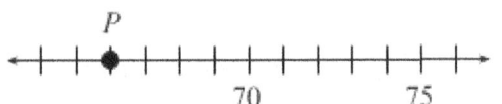

   What number is represented by point P on the number line?

   (A) 64
   (B) 65
   (C) 66
   (D) 67

Go on to the next page. ➤

MA   4

6. A toy company made three toy cars, each with a different power source. The toy cars were tested to see which power source worked best. Each toy car was set to drive in a straight line, and its distance traveled was measured at 5 second intervals. The table shows the collected data.

MODEL CAR DISTANCE EXPERIMENT

Time	Battery	Solar	Rubber Band
0 sec	0 ft	0 ft	0 ft
5 sec	6 ft	6 ft	10 ft
10 sec	12 ft	12 ft	15 ft
15 sec	17 ft	18 ft	17 ft
20 sec	21 ft	24 ft	17 ft

At 10 seconds, how much farther had the rubber band powered toy car traveled than the battery powered car?

(A) 3 feet
(B) 5 feet
(C) 6 feet
(D) 7 feet

---

7. Which fraction is equivalent to 0.6?

(A) $\frac{1}{6}$
(B) $\frac{6}{10}$
(C) $\frac{1}{60}$
(D) $\frac{6}{100}$

8. What is the value of the expression $3,000 - 285$?

(A) 2,515
(B) 2,615
(C) 2,715
(D) 3,615

Go on to the next page. ➤

MA 4

9. The graph shows the size of the graduating class of four high schools.

GRADUATING CLASS SIZE OF FOUR HIGH SCHOOLS

Poly	🎓🎓🎓🎓🎓
North	🎓🎓🎓🎓🎓🎓
Ramona	🎓🎓🎓
King	🎓🎓🎓🎓

🎓 = 200 students

How many more students graduated from Poly than from Ramona?

(A) 200
(B) 400
(C) 800
(D) 1,000

---

10. A basketball court has a total area of 4,700 ft². Which court has an area closest to $\frac{1}{2}$ that of a basketball court?

    (A) a singles tennis court, which has an area of 2,106 ft²
    (B) a badminton court, which has an area of 880 ft²
    (C) a racquetball court, which has an area of 800 ft²
    (D) a ping pong table, which has an area of 45 ft²

11. Use the diagram to answer the question.

    If one of the blocks is picked at random, what is the chance that it will be a ◪ ?

    (A) 1 out of 4
    (B) 1 out of 3
    (C) 1 out of 2
    (D) 2 out of 3

Go on to the next page. ➤

MA

4

12. Use the table to answer the question.

MRS. OPAL'S MATH TEST SCORES

Test 1	98	85	84	87	76
Test 2	97	69	63	78	98
Test 3	98	95	86	85	79
Test 4	84	98	79	92	62

What is the mode of this set of data?

(A) 63
(B) 79
(C) 85
(D) 98

---

13. Use the set of numbers shown to answer the question.

$$\{\,3,\ 5,\ 7,\ 9,\ 11,\ \ldots\,\}$$

Which describes this set of numbers?

(A) prime numbers
(B) even numbers
(C) odd numbers
(D) irrational numbers

14. Which number is divisible by 6 with a remainder of 3?

(A) 18
(B) 19
(C) 20
(D) 21

15. If the area of a rectangle is 24 in², which equation can be used to determine the length of the rectangle? ($A = lw$, where A = Area, l = Length, and w = Width.)

(A) $l = \frac{w}{24}$
(B) $l = \frac{24}{w}$
(C) $l = 24 + w$
(D) $l = 24 - w$

16. Which fraction is between $\frac{2}{3}$ and $\frac{8}{9}$?

(A) $\frac{1}{4}$
(B) $\frac{1}{2}$
(C) $\frac{5}{6}$
(D) $\frac{11}{12}$

Go on to the next page. ➤

MA   4

17. Use the histogram to answer the question.

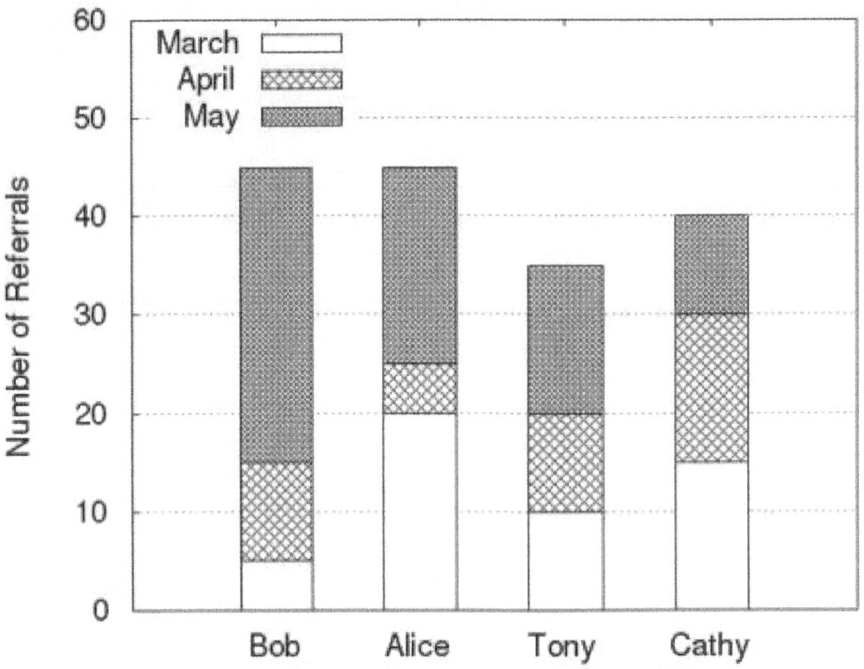

Which employee had the greatest number of referrals during the month of March?

(A) Bob
(B) Alice
(C) Tony
(D) Cathy

---

18. What is the sum of 1.5 and 3.9?

(A) $4\frac{2}{5}$
(B) $5\frac{2}{5}$
(C) $5\frac{3}{5}$
(D) $5\frac{4}{5}$

19. What is the sum of 6.3 and 3.12?

(A) 9.15
(B) 9.42
(C) 10.15
(D) 10.42

Go on to the next page. ➤

MA 4

20. What is the perimeter of a triangle that has side lengths of 5 centimeters, 7 centimeters, and 11 centimeters?
($P = s + s + s$)

(A) 23 centimeters
(B) 24 centimeters
(C) 25 centimeters
(D) 35 centimeters

21. Use the coordinate grid to answer the question.

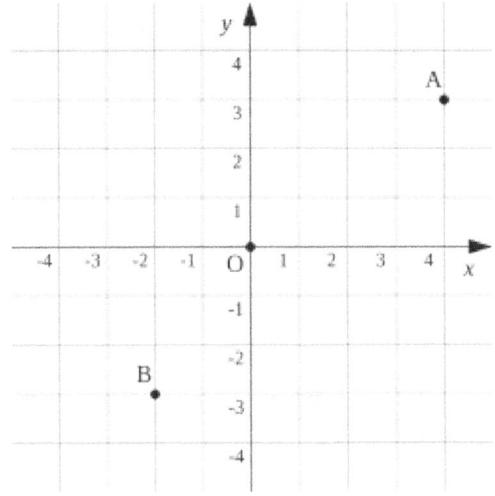

What are the coordinates of point A in the figure?

(A) (4, 3)
(B) (3, 4)
(C) (-2, -3)
(D) (-3, -2)

22. Joseph had $7\frac{3}{4}$ feet of twine. He used $4\frac{7}{8}$ feet of the twine to braid a necklace for his grandmother. How many feet of twine does he have left?

(A) $3\frac{7}{8}$
(B) $2\frac{1}{2}$
(C) $2\frac{3}{4}$
(D) $2\frac{7}{8}$

23. Use the number sequence to answer the question.

1, 7, 13, ___, 25, 31

What is the missing number in the sequence?

(A) 14
(B) 16
(C) 19
(D) 21

24. What is the standard form for seven hundred thirty-two thousand twenty-six?

(A) 73,226
(B) 7,326
(C) 732,026
(D) 732,260

Go on to the next page. ➤

ISEE LL Test #1: Meri-ISEE LL1

MA 4

25. Which fraction is equivalent to 0.25?

    (A) $\frac{3}{12}$
    (B) $\frac{4}{12}$
    (C) $\frac{5}{10}$
    (D) $\frac{1}{8}$

26. Which expression is equal to 40?

    (A) $(5 \times 7) - 3 + 8$
    (B) $5 \times (7 - 3) + 8$
    (C) $5 \times 7 - (3 + 8)$
    (D) $5 \times (7 - 3 + 8)$

27. What is the value of the expression $257 + 108$?

    (A) 305
    (B) 355
    (C) 363
    (D) 365

28. Sean buys five items costing $2.49, $10.99, $0.99, $5.99, and $15.99. What is Sean's estimated total cost?

    (A) between $30 and $35
    (B) between $35 and $40
    (C) between $40 and $45
    (D) between $45 and $50

29. If $3 \times (\square + 2) = 24$, what number does $\square$ stand for?

    (A) 6
    (B) 8
    (C) 10
    (D) 11

30. Use the number sequence to answer the question.

    1, 4, 10, 19, 31, 46, ___

    What is the next number in the sequence?

    (A) 60
    (B) 61
    (C) 63
    (D) 64

STOP.

E 5

Section 5: Essay
30 Minutes

Directions:

You have 30 minutes to plan and write an essay on the topic printed below. Do not write on another topic.

The essay gives you an opportunity to demonstrate your writing skills. The quality of your writing is much more important than the quantity of your writing. Try to express your thoughts clearly and write enough to communicate your ideas.

Please write or print so that your writing may be read by someone who is not familiar with your handwriting.

You may make notes and plan your essay on this page. However, your final response must be on your answer sheet. You must copy the essay topic onto your answer sheet in the box provided.

Please write only the essay topic and final draft of the essay on your answer sheet.

Essay Topic

If you could gain one new skill, what would it be? Explain why you have chosen this skill and how you would put it to use.

STOP.

ISEE LOWER LEVEL TEST #2: MERI-ISEE LL2

VR

Section 1: Verbal Reasoning
34 Questions — 20 Minutes
Part One — Synonyms

Directions: Select the word that is most nearly the same in meaning as the word in capital letters.

1. CUSTODY:

    (A) freedom
    (B) hope
    (C) responsibility
    (D) waste

2. VELOCITY:

    (A) happy
    (B) slow
    (C) speed
    (D) tasty

3. TREACHEROUS:

    (A) helpful
    (B) honest
    (C) tricky
    (D) unworthy

4. ELATED:

    (A) depressed
    (B) jubilant
    (C) quick
    (D) slow

5. EXASPERATE:

    (A) annoy
    (B) appease
    (C) electrifying
    (D) happy

6. DEFT:

    (A) flavorful
    (B) hot
    (C) skillful
    (D) tedious

7. SOOTHE:

    (A) help
    (B) hurt
    (C) pacify
    (D) tolerate

8. IMPROVISE

    (A) destroy
    (B) help
    (C) invent
    (D) plan

Go on to the next page.

VR 1

9. AWE:

   (A) happy
   (B) sad
   (C) shocked
   (D) unfulfilled

10. CHORUS:

    (A) choir
    (B) group
    (C) orchestra
    (D) symphony

11. SKEPTIC:

    (A) believer
    (B) critic
    (C) loyal
    (D) maid

12. OUTMODED:

    (A) crafty
    (B) helpful
    (C) obsolete
    (D) vogue

13. ALTITUDE:

    (A) peak
    (B) swerve
    (C) thermometer
    (D) underground

14. PLAINLY:

    (A) cheaply
    (B) hastily
    (C) noisily
    (D) obviously

15. VERDICT:

    (A) accusation
    (B) arrest
    (C) decree
    (D) jail

16. TENTATIVE:

    (A) cautious
    (B) decisive
    (C) helpful
    (D) unwavering

17. INSISTENT:

    (A) insignificant
    (B) nearsighted
    (C) necessary
    (D) resolute

Go on to the next page. ➤

VR

Part Two — Sentence Completion

Directions: Select the word that best completes the sentence.

18. Mike is usually quite shy when first meeting people, but is much more ------- when you get to know him.

    (A) happy
    (B) hateful
    (C) mean
    (D) sociable

19. The otter is a popular ------- animal found at most local zoos!

    (A) aquatic
    (B) creepy
    (C) strange
    (D) wanted

20. Sarah was sure to ------- the importance of the upcoming test. It was worth at least 60% of her grade!

    (A) emphasize
    (B) feel
    (C) help
    (D) want

21. The hermit crab would ------- from shell to shell, always looking for its next home.

    (A) discourage
    (B) emphasize
    (C) feel
    (D) wander

22. Jack's math teacher's tests were -------; he never knew what was going to be covered on a test!

    (A) difficult
    (B) easy
    (C) sociable
    (D) unpredictable

23. Hannah tried to ------- Sam from eating the old cheese, but Sam still ate the moldy cheese.

    (A) aid
    (B) compel
    (C) discourage
    (D) emphasize

Go on to the next page.

24. What is your -------? Would you go with the brown or white jacket?

    (A) dislike
    (B) edge
    (C) preference
    (D) society

25. Alcatraz was a prison known for holding ------- criminals.

    (A) friendly
    (B) infamous
    (C) nearsighted
    (D) necessary

26. The mountain was ------- from Elena's hotel window, so she would look at it everyday she was on vacation.

    (A) colorful
    (B) incandescent
    (C) obscured
    (D) visible

27. John Smith ------- went to the bank, since he was always scared that something had happened to his money.

    (A) frequently
    (B) happily
    (C) never
    (D) understandably

28. Alison thought about how she could possibly ------- the cake; it was way too dry and the party was starting in less than an hour!

    (A) destroy
    (B) feast
    (C) knead
    (D) moisten

29. Never forget to ------- the cut to make sure to stop the bleeding.

    (A) assure
    (B) compress
    (C) hurt
    (D) navigate

30. It is understandable that Emily didn't understand the new math concepts since she had just -------.

    (A) lost her toy
    (B) helped her mom
    (C) started the lesson
    (D) found a new penny

31. Jessie found 10 dollars while walking home from school, and he -------.

    (A) ran home scared
    (B) looked at his friend
    (C) could not believe his luck
    (D) went swimming at the local pool

VR

32. The squirrels inched closer and closer to the acorn, -------.

    (A) hoping there was a dog nearby
    (B) not caring that it was about to rain
    (C) cautiously watching the nearby cat
    (D) playfully bounding around the yard

33. Joe could not believe how much of a mess there was; -------.

    (A) the room was so clean
    (B) there were people everywhere
    (C) he needed help doing his homework
    (D) it looked like a food fight had just taken place

34. Evan walked around the room in awe; -------.

    (A) he was hungry
    (B) he thought the room was a little plain
    (C) he had trouble concentrating on his test
    (D) he could not believe how big the space was

STOP.

QR

Section 2: Quantitative Reasoning
38 Questions — 35 Minutes

1. A Candy shop sells its sweets by giving customers a bag and allowing them to choose 10 ounces (10 oz) of candy. Tamirah knows that hard candies weigh 1 oz each, gummies weigh 1.5 oz each and taffy weighs 2 oz each. If Tamirah needs at least one hard candy and one taffy, what is the largest number of gummy candies that she can get with her remaining weight allowance?

   (A) 2
   (B) 3
   (C) 4
   (D) 5

2. At the Local Burger Shop, Jaime bought a burger, fries and a milkshake for $18. If the fries cost twice as much as the milkshake, and the burger costs 3 times as much as the milkshake, what did the milkshake cost?

   (A) $2
   (B) $3
   (C) $6
   (D) $9

3. Which of the following quadrilaterals has no axis of symmetry?

   (A) parallelogram
   (B) rectangle
   (C) kite
   (D) rhombus

4. Use the equation below to answer the question.

   $$\tfrac{2}{3}x + 9 = 15$$

   What is the value of x in the equation?

   (A) 4
   (B) 9
   (C) 16
   (D) 36

5. On the bus map, each stop is 2.5 miles apart from the next stop. If Mitch rides from the 6th stop to the 10th stop to get home, then how many miles does he travel?

   (A) 4 miles
   (B) 10 miles
   (C) 15 miles
   (D) 25 miles

Go on to the next page.

QR   2

6. Which of the following equations illustrates the distributive property?

   (A) 13(4 + 10) = (4 + 10)13
   (B) 13(4 + 10) = 13(10 + 4)
   (C) 13(4 + 10) = 13(4 + 10)
   (D) 13(4 + 10) = 13(4) + 13(10)

7. An Animal shelter needs to buy dog food, which costs $2.87 per pound. If the shelter needs 195 pounds of dog food, which of the following is the best estimate for the total cost of the food?

   (A) $600
   (B) $400
   (C) $300
   (D) $200

8. Hoshi knows that his bike can go twice as fast as Sergio's longboard. If Sergio longboards the 2 miles to school in 12 minutes, then how long should it take Hoshi to get to school, if he lives 5 miles away?

   (A) 12
   (B) 15
   (C) 30
   (D) 60

9. What percent of the following numbers are prime numbers?

   11, 12, 13, 14, 15, 16, 17, 18, 19, 20

   (A) 10%
   (B) 20%
   (C) 30%
   (D) 40%

10. Timothy is keeping track of his pet ant colony's population using the following table:

Day	Ant Population
1	27
2	36
4	54
5	63

If the trend continues, how many ants should be in the colony on day 6?

   (A) 60
   (B) 64
   (C) 72
   (D) 80

Go on to the next page. ➤

ISEE LL Test #2: Meri-ISEE LL2

QR 2

11. Yoyneh's favorite trading cards only come in packs of 8, and she just opened enough packs to get 96 new cards. How many more packs must she open if she wants at least 150 cards?

    (A) 6
    (B) 7
    (C) 8
    (D) 18

12. Which of the following expressions is equivalent to $\frac{4}{7} \times \frac{3}{2}$?

    (A) $\frac{4\times 3}{7\times 2}$
    (B) $\frac{4+3}{7+2}$
    (C) $\frac{4\times 2}{7\times 3}$
    (D) $\frac{4+2}{7\times 3}$

13. If the points A(-2,-1), B(2,2), C(-1,6), and D(-5,3) are vertices of a polygon, what type of geometric figure can it be classified as?

    (A) quadrilateral
    (B) square
    (C) parallelogram
    (D) trapezoid

14. If the radius of a circle is doubled, how many times larger will the circumference become?

    (A) 1
    (B) 2
    (C) 3.14
    (D) 4

15. Berg is making a burrito! He will choose one of two types of rice, one of three types of beans, and one of seven types of beans. How many different combinations of rice, beans, and meat could he create for his burrito?

    (A) 3
    (B) 12
    (C) 38
    (D) 42

16. What is the area of the rectangle shown below?

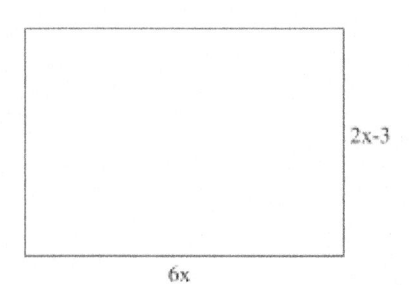

    [rectangle with height $2x-3$ and width $6x$]

    (A) $12x^2 - 18x$
    (B) $12x - 18$
    (C) $16x - 6$
    (D) $8x - 3$

Go on to the next page. ➤

QR

17. Jacques the Landscaper has a bag of seeds that contains 5 iris seeds, 7 daffodil seeds, 8 marigold seeds, and no poppy seeds. Once they are all planted throughout the garden, which plant will make up 40% of the flowers?

    (A) iris
    (B) daffodil
    (C) marigold
    (D) poppy

18. If point A lies on the number line at 3.6 and point B lies on the number line at 9.9, what is the value of point C if it is closer to point A than it is to point B?

    (A) 6.801
    (B) $\sqrt{49}$
    (C) $\frac{34}{5}$
    (D) $\frac{51}{8}$

19. If x is divisible by both 6 and 4, then x is also divisible by which of the following numbers?

    (A) 10
    (B) 12
    (C) 18
    (D) 20

20. What is the perimeter of the following polygon?

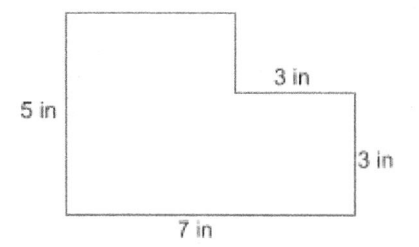

    (A) 18 inches
    (B) 24 inches
    (C) 27 inches
    (D) 29 inches

21. Based on the number line below, what is the sum of A and B?

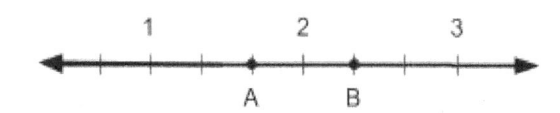

    (A) 0.5
    (B) 2
    (C) 3
    (D) 4

Go on to the next page.

QR

2

22. People were surveyed on whether they prefer dogs, cats, or both as pets and the results are represented in the following venn diagram.

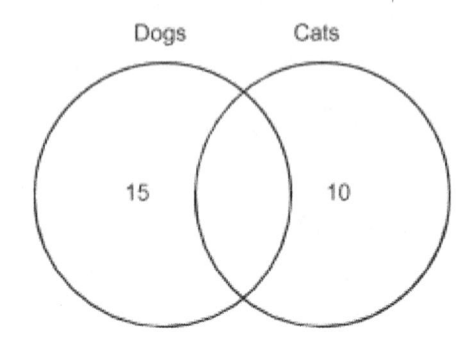

Dogs: 15, Cats: 10

If 32 people were surveyed, how many people stated that they liked both cats and dogs?

(A) 5
(B) 7
(C) 10
(D) 25

23. A bag contains 20 marbles. 12 marbles are blue, 5 are red, and the rest are green. What is the ratio of blue to green marbles in the bag?

(A) 4:1
(B) 3:5
(C) 12:5
(D) 3:2

24. Use the pattern below to answer the question.

ABCDE, ABCED, ABECD, AEBCD...

Which comes next?

(A) EABCD
(B) EDCAB
(C) ABEDC
(D) EDCBA

25. Jeff can walk 8 miles in one hour. David can walk one mile in 10 minutes. Jeff and David have both been walking for one hour. Which statement is TRUE?

(A) David has walked 4 miles farther than Jeff.
(B) David has walked 2 miles farther than Jeff.
(C) Jeff has walked 4 miles farther than David.
(D) Jeff has walked 2 miles farther than David.

26. Which is the largest fraction?

(A) $\frac{18}{27}$
(B) $\frac{4}{7}$
(C) $\frac{15}{25}$
(D) $\frac{7}{13}$

Go on to the next page. ➤

QR

27. The perimeter of an equilateral triangle is 6w. What is the length of one side of the triangle?

    (A) 2
    (B) 3
    (C) 2w
    (D) 3w

28. Which number is exactly halfway between 6.01 and 6.1?

    (A) 6.05
    (B) 6.055
    (C) 6.0555
    (D) 6.06

29. Use the figure below to answer the question.

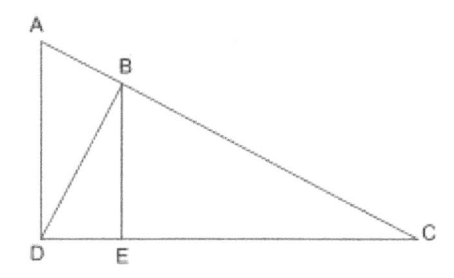

    How many different triangles can be identified in the figure using only the existing lines connecting points A, B, C, D, and E?

    (A) 4
    (B) 5
    (C) 6
    (D) 7

30. In the equation below, what is the value of $2q$?

    $$2q - 2 = q$$

    (A) 0
    (B) 2
    (C) 4
    (D) 5

31. The scale on Katie's map shows that 2 inches equal three miles. On the map, Katie is one foot from her destination. How many miles away is Katie from her destination?

    (A) 6 miles
    (B) 8 miles
    (C) 12 miles
    (D) 18 miles

32. Use the table below to answer the question.

A	B
3	7
6	13
10	21
14	29

    What is the rule for the function?

    (A) $2 \times A + 1 = B$
    (B) $A + 4 = B$
    (C) $3 \times A - 2 = B$
    (D) $A \div 2 + 10 = B$

Go on to the next page. ➤

33. Use the pattern to help answer the question.

$$2^2 + 2 + 3 = 3^2$$
$$3^2 + 3 + 4 = 4^2$$
$$4^2 + 4 + 5 = 5^2$$

What is the value of $a + b$ if $a^2 + 8 + 9 = b^2$?

(A) 17
(B) 72
(C) 81
(D) 145

34. Which of the following is ordered from GREATEST to LEAST?

(A) 0.21, $\frac{1}{5}$, $\frac{4}{15}$, 0.201
(B) 0.201, $\frac{1}{5}$, $\frac{4}{15}$, 0.21
(C) $\frac{1}{5}$, 0.21, 0.201, $\frac{4}{15}$
(D) $\frac{4}{15}$, 0.21, 0.201, $\frac{1}{5}$

35. Use the equations to answer the question.

$$g \times 3 = 9$$
$$f \div 3 = 9$$

What is the product of g and f?

(A) 9
(B) 27
(C) 81
(D) 90

36. Use the diagram below to answer the question.

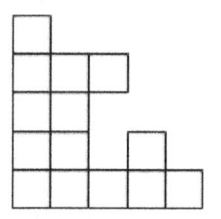

Which of the following would complete the diagram to make a square?

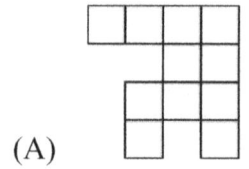

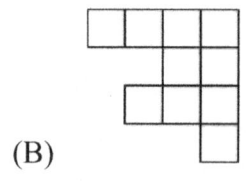

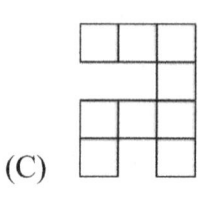

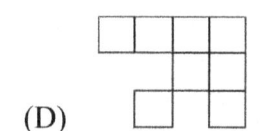

(A)

(B)

(C)

(D)

Go on to the next page.

QR

37. Terry is moving out of his house and is trying to pack up his bookshelf. Terry can fit 15 books into a small moving box. If a large moving box is 2 times wider, 2 times longer, and 3 times taller than a small moving box, how many books can Terry fit into a large moving box?

    (A) 90
    (B) 105
    (C) 150
    (D) 180

38. Which story best fits the equation that follows:

    $$8 \times 3 = 24$$

    (A) A bag of fruit contains 3 apples and 8 oranges. How many pieces of fruit are in the bag?
    (B) One out of every three fruits in a bag is an apple and the rest are oranges. If I have eight apples, how many pieces of fruit are in the bag?
    (C) I have 3 oranges for every apple and 8 apples for every pear. How many more apples are there in my bag than pears?
    (D) 3 oranges cost the same as 8 apples. What is the cost of 3 oranges plus 8 apples?

STOP.

Section 3: Reading Comprehension
25 Questions — 25 Minutes

Questions 1-5

1   Arachnids frighten me, but spiders, those
2 creatures of stealth and death, embody the
3 darkest of my nightmares. Every aspect of
4 their design—their gnarled bodies,
5 venomous mandibles, innumerable eyes, and
6 silken death traps—is terrifyingly surreal.
7 You would think, then, that jumping spiders
8 would elicit in me an overwhelming feeling
9 of horror and dismay. On the contrary,
10 though they retain many of the features of
11 their demonic brethren and can *leap*
12 astonishing distances, I welcome jumping
13 spiders as dear house guests.

14 Many spiders weave complex webs to
15 catch their prey (or my face), but jumping
16 spiders do not. Instead of lazily waiting for
17 prey to come to them, jumping spiders
18 physically hunt down the disgusting pests in
19 my home. Much more efficient and less
20 invasive, I say! Incidentally, jumping
21 spiders are sometimes known to be predators
22 of the notorious brown recluse, one of the
23 few spiders in the U.S. known to be
24 dangerous to humans—yet another reason to
25 celebrate a jumping spider entering your
26 home.

Go on to the next page. ➤

RC   3

1. In line 20, "invasive" most nearly means

   (A) destructive.
   (B) helpful.
   (C) interfering.
   (D) necessary.

2. What is the main idea of this passage?

   (A) All spiders are scary.
   (B) The brown recluse is good to have in your house.
   (C) Jumping spiders are good for your house.
   (D) Spiders are not scary.

3. What can be inferred from the last sentence of the first paragraph (lines 9-13)?

   (A) The narrator hates all bugs.
   (B) The narrator likes jumping spiders.
   (C) The narrator likes all spiders.
   (D) The narrator enjoys finding spiders.

4. The primary purpose of the first paragraph (lines 1-13) is to

   (A) show that spiders are cool.
   (B) show that jumping spiders are helpful.
   (C) show that most spiders are scary.
   (D) show that the brown recluse is dangerous.

5. In line 8, "elicit" most nearly means

   (A) alleviate.
   (B) mitigate.
   (C) provoke.
   (D) suppress.

Go on to the next page. ➤

ISEE LL Test #2: Meri-ISEE LL2   55

Questions 6-10

Bicycles were introduced in the 19th century in Europe, and by the early 21st century, more than 1 billion were in existence at a given time. These numbers far exceed the number of cars in the world, and bicycles are the principal means of transportation in many regions. They also provide a popular form of recreation, and have been adapted for use as children's toys, general fitness, military and police applications, courier services, bicycle racing, and bicycle stunts. The bicycle has truly had a lasting impact around the world.

The "dandy horse", also called Draisienne or Laufmaschine, was the first human means of transport to use only two wheels and was invented by the German Baron Karl von Drais in 1817. It is regarded as the first bicycle, but it did not have pedals. Its rider sat on a wooden frame supported by two in-line wheels and pushed the vehicle along with his or her feet while steering the front wheel.

Several changes and iterations were made by inventors around the world, leading up to the first chain-driven model being developed around 1885. The basic shape and configuration of a typical bicycle has changed little since. However, many details have been improved, especially with the use of more modern materials and computer-aided design.

The bicycle's invention has had an enormous effect on society. In large cities, bicycles have reduced traffic on inner-city streets and reduced crowding in inner-city housing by allowing workers to commute from less crowded homes in the suburbs. In poverty-stricken areas of the world, bicycles can increase a family's income by as much as 35% by contributing to the transport of people and goods. Economically, bicycle manufacturing proved to be a training ground for other industries and led to the development of advanced metalworking techniques, which later enabled metalworkers and mechanics to develop the components used in early automobiles and aircraft. Environmentally, bicycle use has helped to minimize oil consumption. The bicycle is an inexpensive, fast, healthy, and environmentally friendly mode of transport.

Adapted from
Wikipedia contributors, "Bicycle," Wikipedia, The Free Encyclopedia,
https://en.wikipedia.org/w/index.php?title=Bicycle&oldid=947996604 (accessed April 1, 2020).

RC   3

6. What is the main idea of the passage?

   (A) bicycles have had a lasting effect on the world.
   (B) there are many types and styles of bicycles.
   (C) bicycles are an excellent form of exercise.
   (D) the first bicycle was invented in Germany.

7. The primary purpose of the fourth paragraph is to

   (A) suggest further changes that could be made to the bicycle's design.
   (B) discuss how expensive bicycles are in some parts of the world.
   (C) discuss transportation options in inner-cities.
   (D) provide specific examples of how the bicycle has affected society.

8. Which can be inferred from the third paragraph (lines 24-32)?

   (A) All modern bicycles look exactly like those manufactured in 1885.
   (B) Early bicycles were not driven by chains.
   (C) The "dandy horse" is still the most popular bicycle in the world.
   (D) Most bicycles are manufactured in Germany.

9. In line 6, "principal" most nearly means

   (A) primary.
   (B) organizing.
   (C) believing.
   (D) disciplinary.

10. The author's tone in this passage can best be described as

    (A) disgusted.
    (B) ecstatic.
    (C) informative.
    (D) somber.

Go on to the next page. ➤

Questions 11-15

Deep within the Earth it is so hot that some rocks slowly melt and become a thick flowing substance called magma. Since it is lighter than the solid rock around it, magma rises and collects in magma chambers. Eventually, some of the magma pushes through vents and fissures to the Earth's surface. Magma that has erupted is called lava.

Some volcanic eruptions are explosive and others are not. The explosivity of an eruption depends on the composition of the magma. If magma is thin and runny, gases can escape easily from it. When this type of magma erupts, it flows out of the volcano. A good example is the eruptions at Hawaii's volcanoes. Lava flows rarely kill people because they move slowly enough for people to get out of their way. If magma is thick and sticky, gases cannot escape easily. Pressure builds up until the gases escape violently and explode. A good example is the eruption of Washington's Mount St. Helens. In this type of eruption, the magma blasts into the air and breaks apart into pieces called tephra. Tephra can range in size from tiny particles of ash to house-size boulders.

Explosive volcanic eruptions can be dangerous and deadly. They can blast out clouds of hot tephra from the side or top of a volcano. These fiery clouds race down mountainsides destroying almost everything in their path. Ash erupted into the sky falls back to Earth like powdery snow. If thick enough, blankets of ash can suffocate plants, animals, and humans. When hot volcanic materials mix with water from streams or melted snow and ice, mudflows form. Mudflows have buried entire communities located near erupting volcanoes.

Public Domain
"How Do Volcanoes Erupt?," U.S. Geological Survey, https://www.usgs.gov/faqs/how-do-volcanoes-erupt?qt-news_science_products=0#qt-news_science_products (accessed April 1, 2020)

RC

3

11. What determines the explosivity of volcanic eruptions?

    (A) the temperature within a volcano
    (B) the size of the tephra involved in the eruption
    (C) the number of vents and fissures around the volcano
    (D) the composition of the magma

12. The author would most likely agree with which of the following?

    (A) Volcanic eruptions are always deadly.
    (B) Mudflows can be just as deadly as the eruptions themselves.
    (C) Lava flows always move too quickly for people to get out of their way.
    (D) All mountains are active volcanoes.

13. An explosive eruption is most likely to happen if

    (A) the magma is thin and runny.
    (B) the magma is thick and sticky.
    (C) a volcano has not erupted in a long time.
    (D) a volcano is very large.

14. This passage would most likely appear in

    (A) a diary.
    (B) a newspaper.
    (C) a science fiction novel.
    (D) a textbook.

15. As used in line 12, "composition" most nearly means

    (A) makeup.
    (B) control.
    (C) physical shape.
    (D) architecture.

Go on to the next page. ➤

Questions 16-20

At the end of what seemed a tedious while, I had managed to pack my head full of islands, towns, bars, "points," and bends; and a curiously inanimate mass of lumber it was, too. However, inasmuch as I could shut my eyes, and reel off a good long string of these names without leaving out more than ten miles of river in every fifty, I began to feel that I could take a boat down to New Orleans if I could make her skip those little gaps. But of course my complacency could hardly get start enough to lift my nose a trifle into the air, before Mr. Bixby would think of something to fetch it down again. One day he turned on me suddenly with this settler—

"What is the shape of Walnut Bend?"

He might as well have asked me my grandmother's opinion of protoplasm. I reflected respectfully, and then said I didn't know it had any particular shape. My gunpowdery chief went off with a bang, of course, and then went on loading and firing until he was out of adjectives.

I had learned long ago that he only carried just so many rounds of ammunition, and was sure to subside into a very placable and even remorseful old smooth-bore as soon as they were all gone. That word "old" is merely affectionate; he was not more than thirty-four. I waited.

Adapted from
Life On The Mississippi, Complete by Mark Twain (Samuel Clemens)
https://www.gutenberg.org/files/245/245-h/245-h.htm

16. As used in line 4, "curiously" most nearly means

(A) explosive.
(B) loud.
(C) smokey.
(D) strangely.

17. The tone of the passage can best be described as

(A) amazement.
(B) despair.
(C) humorous.
(D) serious.

18. The passage can best be described as

(A) propaganda.
(B) an autobiography.
(C) a research report.
(D) a textbook excerpt.

19. As used in line 6, "reel off" most nearly means

(A) list.
(B) pull.
(C) push.
(D) unwind.

20. In line 18, the author uses the phrase "grandmother's opinion of protoplasm" in order to

(A) show that he understands what Mr. Bixby is asking.
(B) show that he doesn't understand what Mr. Bixby is asking him.
(C) show that his grandmother knows about protoplasm.
(D) introduce his grandmother's opinion on protoplasm.

Questions 21-25

Henry Ford was an American industrialist and business leader, founder of the Ford Motor Company, and chief developer of the assembly line technique of mass production. By creating the first automobile that middle-class Americans could afford, he changed the automobile from an expensive luxury into an accessible means of transportation that would change the landscape of the 20th century.

The Model T was introduced on October 1, 1908. The car was affordable, very simple to drive, and easy and cheap to repair. It was so cheap that by the 1920s, most American drivers had learned to drive on the Model T. Ford created a huge marketing effort to ensure that newspapers carried stories and ads about the new product, and Ford's network of local automobile dealers made the car ubiquitous in almost every city in North America.

By 1918, half of all cars in the United States were Model Ts. Until the development of the assembly line, which mandated black paint because of its quicker drying time, Model Ts were available in other colors. However, all newer cars were black; as Ford wrote in his autobiography, "Any customer can have a car painted any color that he wants so long as it is black." The decision was strongly defended by Ford, and production of the Model T continued as late as 1927; the final total production was 15,007,034 over 19 years, a record that stood for the next 45 years.

Ford's introduction of the Model T automobile revolutionized transportation and American industry. His goals of mass production of inexpensive goods, high wages for workers, and lowering production costs resulted in many technical and business innovations, including the assembly line and franchise dealership system.

Adapted from
Wikipedia contributors, "Henry Ford," Wikipedia, The Free Encyclopedia,
https://en.wikipedia.org/w/index.php?title=Henry_Ford&oldid=947493120 (accessed April 2, 2020).

21. The primary purpose of the passage is to

    (A) summarize the life of Henry Ford.
    (B) describe the Model T manufacturing process.
    (C) explain the significance of the Model T for transportation.
    (D) list the various innovations that resulted from the Model T.

22. The passage implies that the primary reason for the Model T's popularity was that it was

    (A) fast.
    (B) reliable.
    (C) painted black.
    (D) affordable.

23. In line 20, "ubiquitous" most nearly means

    (A) loved.
    (B) sold.
    (C) present.
    (D) manufactured.

24. In what year did the production of the Model T end?

    (A) 1927
    (B) 1920
    (C) 1918
    (D) 1908

25. Why were all Model Ts that were built on an assembly line painted black?

    (A) Black was Henry Ford's favorite color.
    (B) Black paint dried more quickly than other colors.
    (C) Black was the most popular color even when other colors were offered
    (D) Black was the winner of a newspaper survey.

Section 4: Mathematics Achievement
30 Questions — 30 Minutes

1. Which of the following is the standard form for two hundred thousand four hundred six?

    (A) 246,000
    (B) 204,006
    (C) 200,406
    (D) 200,046

2. If Joey buys two carrots for $0.50 each, and three apples, and he spent $2.23, how much did each apple cost?

    (A) $0.23
    (B) $0.41
    (C) $0.52
    (D) $0.56

3. The probability of pulling a red marble from a bag of red, white, and blue marbles is 2/3. If there are twice as many blue marbles as white marbles, and there are six red marbles in the bag, how many white marbles can there be?

    (A) 1
    (B) 2
    (C) 3
    (D) 4

4. Which of the following is an improper fraction?

    (A) $\frac{1}{3}$
    (B) $\frac{2}{3}$
    (C) $\frac{3}{3}$
    (D) $\frac{4}{3}$

5. Sandy has a cat. If she wants to measure how long the cat is, what are the most appropriate units?

    (A) inches
    (B) pounds
    (C) gallons
    (D) miles

6. $\frac{1}{5} + \frac{1}{2} =$

    (A) $\frac{1}{10}$
    (B) $\frac{2}{3}$
    (C) $\frac{4}{3}$
    (D) $\frac{7}{10}$

7. What is thirty percent of 50?

    (A) 10
    (B) 15
    (C) 30
    (D) 45

Go on to the next page. ➤

8. Which of the following describes a four-sided shape which has exactly two parallel sides?

(A) trapezoid
(B) square
(C) rhombus
(D) kite

9. Kim had 12 donuts. She ate one third of them, and then gave away half of the remaining donuts. How many does she have left over?

(A) 0
(B) 1
(C) 3
(D) 4

10. $(9 \div 3) + 14 \times 2 =$

(A) 5
(B) 10
(C) 30
(D) 31

11. What is the value of the units digit of the number 2010.298?

(A) 0
(B) 1
(C) 2
(D) 9

Questions 12-14 refer to the table below.

Number of Pears Sold per Store on Wednesday

Note: 🍐 =10 pears

Jason's Groceries	🍐🍐🍐🍐
Entire Eats	🍐🍐🍐
Alto Wholesalers	🍐🍐🍐🍐🍐🍐
Merchant Jeffrey's	🍐🍐

12. How many pears were sold at the store that sold the least number of pears on Wednesday?

(A) 2
(B) 10
(C) 20
(D) 30

13. What was the average number of pears sold on Wednesday at all of the stores?

(A) 30.5
(B) 37.5
(C) 41.5
(D) 65.5

14. How many more pears were sold at Jason's Groceries than Merchant Jeffrey's?

(A) 2
(B) 3
(C) 20
(D) 45

Go on to the next page. ➤

Questions 15-16 refer to the following graph.

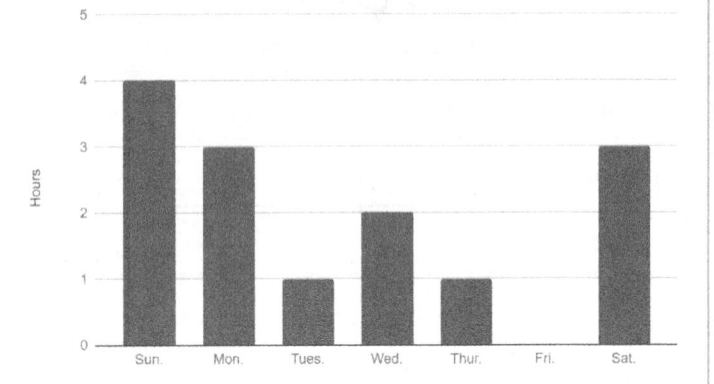

Hours Spent Driving on Vacation

15. On average, how many hours were spent driving on vacation per day?

    (A) 2.0
    (B) 2.5
    (C) 3.0
    (D) 4.0

16. On which day was more driving done than on Monday?

    (A) Sunday
    (B) Tuesday
    (C) Thursday
    (D) Saturday

17. What is $\frac{2}{5}$ of 10?

    (A) 4
    (B) 5
    (C) 8
    (D) 10

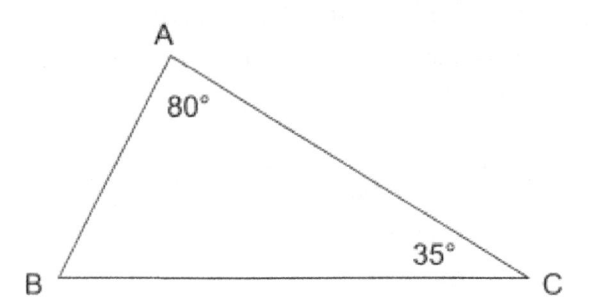

18. What is the degree measure of $\angle ABC$?

    (A) 50
    (B) 65
    (C) 90
    (D) 130

19. All of the following are multiples of 5 EXCEPT

    (A) 25
    (B) 55
    (C) 166
    (D) 1660

20. $\frac{14}{21} \div \frac{14}{7} =$

    (A) $\frac{1}{4}$
    (B) $\frac{6}{21}$
    (C) $\frac{1}{3}$
    (D) $\frac{4}{3}$

21. $10 \times 15 + 5 =$

    (A) 100
    (B) 155
    (C) 200
    (D) 255

Go on to the next page. ➤

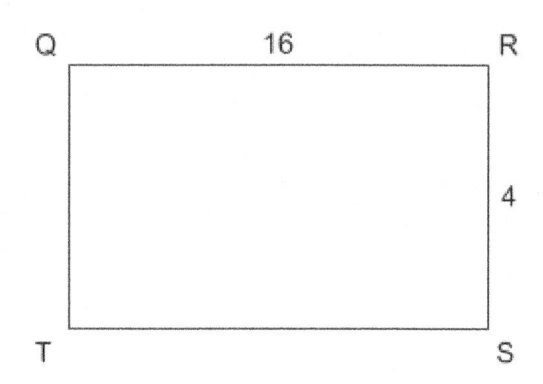

MA 4

[Rectangle QRST with QR = 16, RS = 4]

22. What is the area of rectangle QRST shown above?

    (A) 16
    (B) 40
    (C) 64
    (D) 128

Apple prices
Red Delicious................$1.00 per lb
Granny Smith....................$0.75 per lb
Fuji...........................$1.15 per lb

23. Jenny has $12.50 to spend on apples. If she knows she wants to spend $6.90 on Fuji apples, how many pounds of Granny Smith apples can she buy if she wants four pounds of Red Delicious apples? Round your answer to the nearest whole number.

    (A) 0
    (B) 1
    (C) 2
    (D) 3

Questions 24-25 refer to the following table.

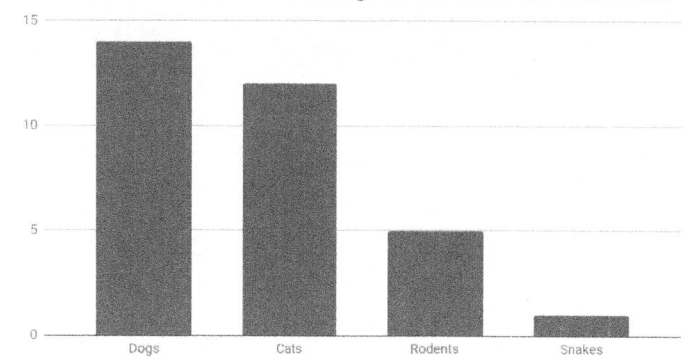

Students with Each of the Following Animals in the 6th Grade Class

[Bar chart showing Dogs ~14, Cats ~12, Rodents ~5, Snakes ~1]

24. Which of the following is closest to the difference between the number of students with cats and the number of students with rodents?

    (A) 1
    (B) 5
    (C) 7
    (D) 10

25. Which of the four categories of animals occurs the least of all the categories?

    (A) snakes
    (B) rodents
    (C) cats
    (D) dogs

26. $40 \div 4 = 5 + \blacksquare$, what is $\blacksquare$?

    (A) 1
    (B) 3
    (C) 5
    (D) 10

Go on to the next page. ➤

MA
4

27. How many more hours is $9\frac{1}{3}$ hours than $7\frac{1}{2}$ hours?

   (A) $1\frac{1}{6}$
   (B) $1\frac{5}{6}$
   (C) 2
   (D) $2\frac{5}{7}$

Questions 28-30 refer to the following table.

Cost per Ticket at Various Times at the Movie Theater

	CHILD (UNDER 12)	**STUDENT (14-18)**	**ADULT (OVER 18)**
Weekend Matinee	$4.00	$9.00	$12.00
Mon. - Thur.	$5.00	$9.00	$12.00
Weekend Evening	$6.50	$12.00	$15.00

28. If three children and two adults go to the movies on a Tuesday, how much will they need to pay?

   (A) $10.10
   (B) $29.00
   (C) $38.50
   (D) $39.00

29. How much more does it cost for a Student and Adult to see a movie on a Weekend Evening than a Child and Adult?

   (A) $4.50
   (B) $4.75
   (C) $5.00
   (D) $5.50

30. If Tony is 35 years old, and his two daughters, Alicia and Annie are 5 years old and 7 years old respectively, how much will they all have to pay to see a movie during the Weekend Matinee?

   (A) $13.00
   (B) $15.00
   (C) $20.00
   (D) $30.00

STOP.

E

5

Section 5: Essay

30 Minutes

Directions:

You have 30 minutes to plan and write an essay on the topic printed below. Do not write on another topic.

The essay gives you an opportunity to demonstrate your writing skills. The quality of your writing is much more important than the quantity of your writing. Try to express your thoughts clearly and write enough to communicate your ideas.

Please write or print so that your writing may be read by someone who is not familiar with your handwriting.

You may make notes and plan your essay on this page. However, your final response must be on your answer sheet. You must copy the essay topic onto your answer sheet in the box provided.

Please write only the essay topic and final draft of the essay on your answer sheet.

Essay Topic

What is your favorite subject in school? Explain why this subject is your favorite.

STOP.

ISEE LOWER LEVEL TEST #3: MERI-ISEE LL3

Section 1: Verbal Reasoning
34 Questions — 20 Minutes
Part One — Synonyms

Directions: Select the word that is most nearly the same in meaning as the word in capital letters.

---

1. ABDICATE:

    (A) conquer
    (B) defend
    (C) forfeit
    (D) strain

2. CANINE:

    (A) animal
    (B) dog
    (C) feline
    (D) bite

3. DEBRIS:

    (A) bush
    (B) gem
    (C) prize
    (D) waste

4. HARSH:

    (A) excited
    (B) kind
    (C) relaxing
    (D) severe

5. ILLITERATE:

    (A) careful
    (B) ignorant
    (C) instructional
    (D) wise

6. HUMID:

    (A) dry
    (B) dusty
    (C) hot
    (D) moist

7. HOVEL:

    (A) limp
    (B) origin
    (C) shelter
    (D) shovel

8. CELESTIAL:

    (A) earthly
    (B) heavenly
    (C) hot
    (D) worldly

Go on to the next page. ➤

VR

9. AMPHIBIAN:

   (A) bacteria
   (B) fish
   (C) frog
   (D) reptile

10. SENTRY:

    (A) artist
    (B) doctor
    (C) soldier
    (D) thinker

11. REGAL:

    (A) average
    (B) humble
    (C) mean
    (D) royal

12. LAGOON:

    (A) beach
    (B) desert
    (C) stranded
    (D) swamp

13. NAUSEOUS:

    (A) healthy
    (B) settled
    (C) sick
    (D) well

14. DESPICABLE:

    (A) clean
    (B) good
    (C) proud
    (D) shameful

15. ZEALOUS:

    (A) enthusiastic
    (B) heated
    (C) sad
    (D) upset

16. RANDOM:

    (A) chance
    (B) decided
    (C) planned
    (D) regular

17. PEDESTRIAN:

    (A) amazing
    (B) every-day
    (C) interesting
    (D) moving

Go on to the next page. ➤

VR

Part Two — Sentence Completion

Directions: Select the word that best completes the sentence.

18. The teacher accused Alex and Terry of ------- because they turned in the same essay, each claiming the essay as their own.

    (A) marking up
    (B) original work
    (C) plagiarism
    (D) printing

19. Students on the field trip ------- in amazement at the herd of elephants running through the enclosure at the Wild Animal Park.

    (A) gandered
    (B) glanced
    (C) glimpsed
    (D) marveled

20. The sweet ------- of the baking cookies wafted through the entire house.

    (A) aroma
    (B) odor
    (C) stench
    (D) tunes

21. Cheetahs, capable of ------- up to 75 mph, are famous for their extreme speed.

    (A) lateness
    (B) procrastinations
    (C) torpidity
    (D) velocities

22. After spending two days lost in the desert with no food or water, the starving hikers ------- the snacks the park rangers handed them on the drive to the station.

    (A) conserved
    (B) devoured
    (C) nibbled
    (D) saved

23. -------, Martha trudged back home after Calvin smashed the cupcakes she had spent days perfecting to compete with on Cupcake Wars.

    (A) Devastated
    (B) Patched
    (C) Recovered
    (D) Restored

Go on to the next page.

VR 1

24. The ------- comment reduced Kayla to tears.

    (A) abhorrent
    (B) civil
    (C) inoffensive
    (D) kind

25. Fishermen ------- buoys to underwater gear used to catch deep sea creatures, such as lobsters and crabs.

    (A) divide
    (B) float
    (C) loosen
    (D) tether

26. By stealing fire from the gods to give to man, Prometheus unleashed the ------- of Zeus.

    (A) forbearance
    (B) love
    (C) pardon
    (D) wrath

27. In order to ------- an amendment, the amendment must first pass the House and Senate by a two-thirds vote; then, the amendment is sent to the states where three-quarters must pass the amendment.

    (A) neglect
    (B) ratify
    (C) refuse
    (D) spurn

28. -------, according to Merriam Webster, is defined as "exempt from death" or "lasting forever."

    (A) immortal
    (B) mortal
    (C) short-term
    (D) temporary

29. Even after arguing for what seemed like hours, Tom and Jerry could not settle their -------.

    (A) concord
    (B) dispute
    (C) harmony
    (D) peace

30. In joint effort, zoologists, nutritionists and ------- work together to help create varied plant-filled diets for the vegetarian residents of the San Diego Zoo.

    (A) botanists
    (B) dermatologists
    (C) geologists
    (D) philanthropists

31. Cause is to reason as ------- is to consequence.

    (A) conservation
    (B) effect
    (C) responsibility
    (D) weakness

VR

32. Astronauts living on the International Space Station -------.

    (A) go shopping
    (B) orbit around Earth
    (C) converse with extraterrestrials
    (D) float through space on a random trajectory

33. -------, Tonya and Nancy faced off at the tennis match, each fighting to win the gold medal.

    (A) Best friends
    (B) Sympathetic athletes
    (C) Empathetic colleagues
    (D) Competitive adversaries

34. After realizing he had ruined Dr. Fitzherbert's career-long experiment testing a hypothesis of string theory, Carl admitted he'd only had a ------- of what Fitzherbert had asked him to test.

    (A) vague idea
    (B) certain idea
    (C) definite understanding
    (D) complete understanding

STOP.

Section 2: Quantitative Reasoning
38 Questions — 35 Minutes

1. Wendy is baking a cake for her friends. For a small cake, she needs 3 cups of flour, 1 cup of sugar, and 2 cups of eggs. If a large cake uses 24 total cups of ingredients in the same ratio, how many cups of flour does she need to make a large cake?

   (A) 12
   (B) 15
   (C) 18
   (D) 21

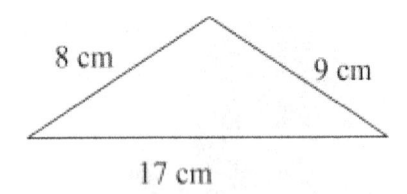

2. What is the perimeter of the triangle above?

   (A) 17 cm
   (B) 25 cm
   (C) 26 cm
   (D) 34 cm

3. If v is divisible by both 2 and 5, which of the following must v also be divisible by?

   (A) 4
   (B) 7
   (C) 10
   (D) 25

4. Which of the following is the product of two distinct prime numbers?

   (A) 25
   (B) 15
   (C) 9
   (D) 5

5. Which of these is sixteen thousand forty three?

   (A) 1,643
   (B) 16,403
   (C) 16,043
   (D) 160,043

6. Which of the following is the best estimate for the product of 507 and 28?

   (A) 500 + 30
   (B) 550 × 30
   (C) 500 × 30
   (D) 600 × 20

7. What is the sum of the distinct prime factors of 28?

   (A) 9
   (B) 10
   (C) 11
   (D) 16

Go on to the next page.

QR

8. How much more is ⅔ than ½ ?

    (A) ⅓
    (B) ⅕
    (C) ⅙
    (D) ⅛

9. Elizabeth has 4 feet of yarn. If she cuts them into 3-inch pieces, how many pieces can she make?
    Note: 1 foot = 12 inches

    (A) 16
    (B) 12
    (C) 8
    (D) 4

10. Which of the following is NOT a prime number?

    (A) 5
    (B) 4
    (C) 3
    (D) 2

11. In a bag, there are 20 marbles. There are 6 striped marbles, 5 solid-colored marbles, and the rest are clear. What percentage of the marbles are clear?

    (A) 55 percent
    (B) 45 percent
    (C) 11 percent
    (D) 9 percent

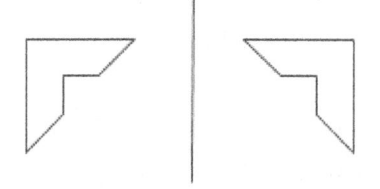

12. Which of the following transformations could be performed to get the figure on the left to match with the figure on the right?

    (A) Slide the figure to the right without turning it
    (B) Rotate the figure 180° about it's top left corner
    (C) Reflect across the line in the middle
    (D) Dilate the figure to be twice as large

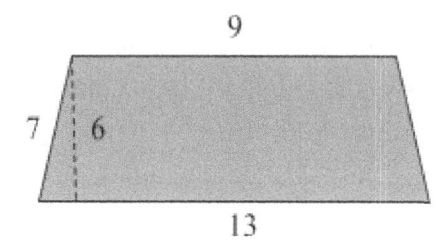

13. What is the area of the figure shown above?

    (A) 54
    (B) 66
    (C) 77
    (D) 78

Go on to the next page. ➤

QR 2

14. What is the side length of the square whose area is 36 square inches?

    (A) 6 feet
    (B) 6 inches
    (C) 9 inches
    (D) 18 inches

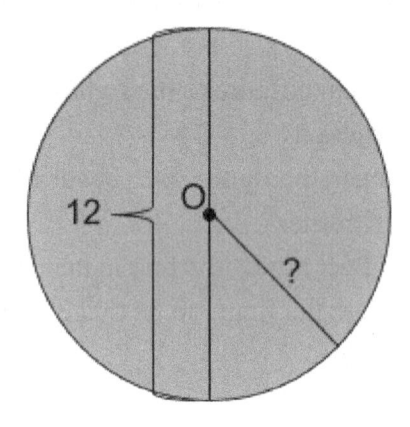

15. If point O is the center of the circle above, what is the length of the segment from O to the edge of the circle?
    Note: this is called the radius.

    (A) 12
    (B) 10
    (C) 8
    (D) 6

16. The price of a steak is $27, while the price of a plate of chicken is $13. How much more expensive are 2 steaks than 3 chicken plates?

    (A) $14
    (B) $15
    (C) $28
    (D) $42

17. Which of the following is closest to 74?

    (A) 74.8
    (B) 74.08
    (C) 74.008
    (D) 74.081

18. Dr. Stoll bikes 5 miles in 15 minutes. At this rate, how long will it take him to ride 8 miles?

    (A) 20 minutes
    (B) 22 minutes
    (C) 24 minutes
    (D) 25 minutes

19. Each serving of rice requires ¾ cup of rice. If we have a bag with 12 cups of rice, how many servings are in this bag?

    (A) 16
    (B) 11
    (C) 9
    (D) 8

Go on to the next page. ➤

QR 2

20. On a trip to the grocery store, you buy the following items in the quantity specified. Which of the following is the best approximate of the total of your groceries without tax?

Item	Unit Price	Quantity
Cereal	$3.99 / box	2 boxes
Ground Turkey	$4.51 / lb	4 pounds
Carrots	$1.99 / lb	1 pound

(A) $10.50
(B) $19.00
(C) $24.00
(D) $28.00

21. When a number is divided by 2, and then divided by 3, the remainder is 1. Which of these could be the number?

(A) 12
(B) 13
(C) 14
(D) 15

22. Which of the following displays the prime factorization of 12?

(A) 3×4
(B) 2×6
(C) $2 \times 2 \times 3$
(D) $2 \times 3 \times 3$

23. In the multiplication problem below, if T is a positive digit, what is the value of T?

$$\begin{array}{r} T \\ \times T \\ \hline 3T \end{array}$$

(A) 4
(B) 5
(C) 6
(D) 7

24. Max is working at a car wash, and usually makes $60 per day. On a certain day, he makes 25% extra. How much extra money, in dollars, did Max earn on this day?

(A) 15
(B) 20
(C) 25
(D) 30

25. Selma has 4 children, and just bought a pack of 45 apples. If she gives one to each of her children for a week, how many apples will she have left over?

(A) 1
(B) 17
(C) 21
(D) 28

Go on to the next page. ➤

QR

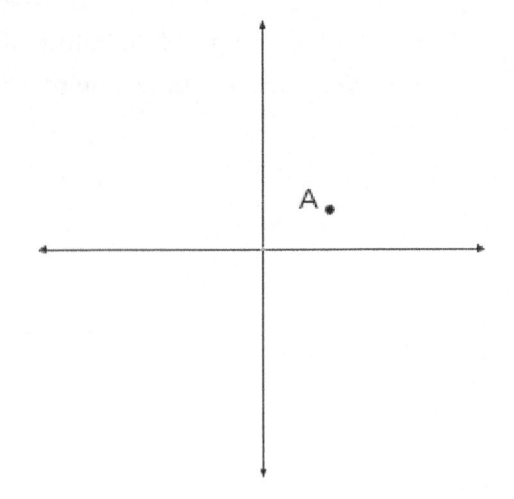

26. Which of the following could be the coordinates of point A?
    (A) (0, 0)
    (B) (1, -2)
    (C) (2, 1)
    (D) (2, -1)

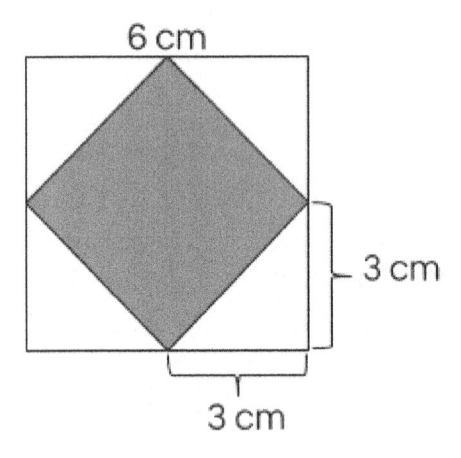

27. The figure above displays a square with side lengths of 6cm. If the 3cm by 3cm triangles are cut from the square, what is the area of the remaining diamond?
    (A) 9 cm²
    (B) 18 cm²
    (C) 27 cm²
    (D) 30 cm²

28. The chance of pulling a red card from a pile of cards is 3 out of 8. Which of the following could be the number of red cards and other cards?

    (A) 3 red cards and 8 others
    (B) 6 red cards and 16 others
    (C) 6 red cards and 10 others
    (D) 5 red cards and 3 others

29. How many ways are there to mix up the letters in the word DOG?

    (A) 3
    (B) 4
    (C) 5
    (D) 6

30. Jackson wants to buy a $500 TV. If he has to pay a 10% tax on his purchase, how much must he pay in all?

    (A) $50
    (B) $55
    (C) $550
    (D) $555

31. Bryce is a baseball player who says he can hit 30 home runs every season, and thinks he will play for 17 seasons as a professional. If he does this, how many home runs will he have when he retires?

    (A) 470
    (B) 510
    (C) 540
    (D) 600

Go on to the next page.

QR

32. When trying to see how many licks to get to the center of a lollipop, you discover that 30 licks gets rid of ⅛ of an inch. If the lollipop is 1 ½ inches in diameter, how many licks does it take to get to the exact center?

    (A) 180
    (B) 240
    (C) 290
    (D) 360

33. At the beginning of the day, the temperature was 63 degrees. At noon, the temperature rose by 18 degrees. By nightfall, the temperature was 21 degrees cooler than at noon. What was the temperature at nightfall?

    (A) 103 degrees
    (B) 81 degrees
    (C) 63 degrees
    (D) 60 degrees

34. Approximately how much more is it to buy 12 individual magazines at $2.99 each than to get a yearly subscription for $14.99?

    (A) $21
    (B) $15
    (C) $13
    (D) $3

35. Which of the following is the largest?

    (A) 0.578
    (B) 0.580
    (C) 57.9 %
    (D) 60.5 %

36. 4 friends decide to eat 3 pizzas together. If each pizzas is cut into 8 equal slices and each friend eats an equal amount, how many slices will each person eat?

    (A) 6
    (B) 8
    (C) 10
    (D) 12

37. Elliott wants to make money for a new game that costs $60 by shoveling snow from driveways. He has $5 right now, and needs to shovel 5 driveways to have enough for the game. How much does he charge to shovel a driveway?

    (A) $11
    (B) $10
    (C) $6
    (D) $5

Go on to the next page. ➤

QR 2

38. An ant wants to walk around a small board labeled below. The board is made up of two congruent triangles. How far must the and walk to go all the way around every edge?

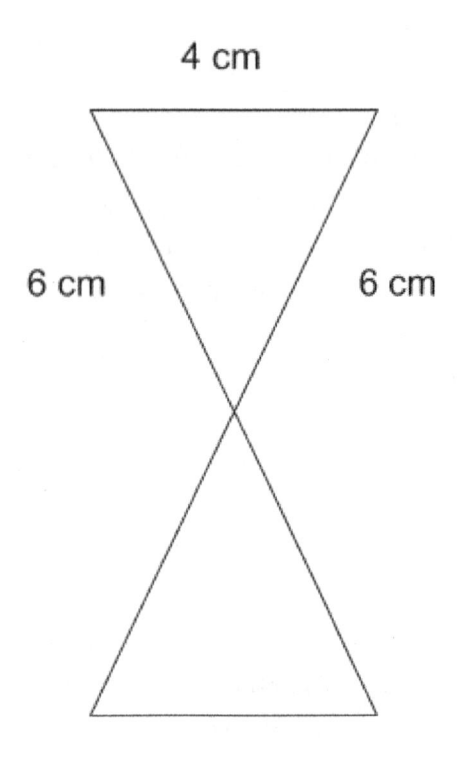

4 cm

6 cm   6 cm

(A) 12 cm
(B) 16 cm
(C) 24 cm
(D) 32 cm

STOP.

Section 3: Reading Comprehension
25 Questions — 25 Minutes

Questions 1-5

1 Any given animal can seem unique if
2 one really thinks about it, but one animal
3 that truly sets itself apart is the sloth. The
4 sloth is special for its speed—its lack of
5 speed, that is. In fact, the slowest animal on
6 earth is the three-toed sloth.
7   Sloths barely move at all, but when they
8 do, they are remarkably slow. When they are
9 at their fastest, like when getting away
10 from a predator, sloths travel at about 15
11 feet per minute. Compare that number to
12 450 feet per minute, which is a human
13 jogging, and not very fast.
14   A sloth will spend almost its entire life
15 hanging upside-down. The hands, feet, and
16 arms of sloths are adapted to allow them to
17 hang from tree limbs easily. Sloths eat,
18 sleep, and even give birth hanging
19 upside-down on tree limbs. When on the
20 ground, sloths cannot really walk—they
21 mostly drag themselves across the ground. If
22 a sloth were ever to find itself in water,
23 however, it would be able to swim quite fast
24 at about 44 feet per minute.
25   Sloths also have the uncommon situation
26 of having algae grow on their fur. Algae
27 usually live in the ocean, but they seem to be
28 able to grow on the fur of sloths because
29 sloths move so slowly. Interestingly, the
30 algae actually help to protect sloths from
31 predators by helping them blend in with the
32 trees in which they live.
33   Sloths not only move slowly, they also
34 digest their food slowly. As a result, they
35 only need to go to the bathroom about once
36 a week. They climb down all the way to the
37 ground, where they are vulnerable to
38 predators, and always go to the same spot
39 every time. No one knows why they do this.
40   Indeed, there is much to wonder about
41 when it comes to sloths.

Go on to the next page. ➢

RC

3

1. The primary purpose of this passage is to

   (A) discuss several types of animals that are similar to sloths.
   (B) explain how sloths are different from other animals.
   (C) describe the origin of the name "sloth."
   (D) compare sloths with other tree-climbing animals.

2. Which word is closest in meaning to "vulnerable" (line 37)?

   (A) decent
   (B) defenseless
   (C) ferocious
   (D) valuable

3. According to the third paragraph (lines 14-24), it can be inferred that

   (A) sloths move at the same speed at all times.
   (B) sloths move faster or slower depending on where they are.
   (C) sloths are as comfortable on the ground as they are hanging upside-down.
   (D) sloths live both in the jungle and in the ocean.

4. The passage answers which of these following questions?

   (A) Where is the three-toed sloth's natural habitat?
   (B) How many babies do sloths give birth to at one time?
   (C) How does algae protect sloths?
   (D) Are sloths communal or solitary animals?

5. The author's attitude toward the sloths is best described as

   (A) alarmed.
   (B) distant.
   (C) fascinated.
   (D) indifferent.

Go on to the next page. ➤

Questions 6-10

On January 20, 1961, John F. Kennedy took the oath of office to become the 35th president of the United States of America. That day, President Kennedy gave one of the most famous inaugural addresses in U.S. history. Through his speech, the new president aimed to inspire the American people to engage in civic action and public service, just as he was about to do in the highest office in the land.

In his inaugural speech, President Kennedy discussed issues both domestic and foreign. He spoke about freedom, liberty, and morality. His listeners could ascertain that he was concerned about hunger, poverty, and nuclear war, and his solution was for all people to work together with a united hope for peace and justice.

The most famous line from his speech shows how he wanted his compatriots to take action instead of sitting around expecting results: "And so, my fellow Americans: ask not what your country can do for you—ask what you can do for your country." He said that the success or failure of the world was more in the hands of the citizens than in his own.

He also continued by addressing the rest of the world. To his most famous line he added, "My fellow citizens of the world: ask not what America will do for you, but what together we can do for the freedom of man." He was asking the whole world to help bring peace and freedom, as if he knew for certain that Americans would never be able to do it alone.

President Kennedy had not won his election easily; therefore, he knew how important his inaugural speech would be. He put enormous effort into crafting his speech, asking for the help of his friend, Ted Sorenson, who became his chief legislative aide. It is said that for days, Kennedy carried a paper copy of his speech to review it as much as he could, even at the breakfast table before his inauguration.

After President Kennedy had successfully delivered his speech, his approval ratings went up dramatically. He even inspired schoolchildren to write him letters. A third grader from Florida named Brenda Sue Wesson said that after the students in her class saw Kennedy's inauguration on T.V., they knew he would be their best president.

RC

3

6. Which sentence best expresses the primary purpose of this passage?

   (A) President Kennedy had a good relationship with his chief legislative aide, Ted Sorenson.
   (B) President Kennedy's inaugural speech was mainly targeted to the whole world.
   (C) Many people thought that President Kennedy's speech was difficult to understand.
   (D) President Kennedy's inaugural speech helped him to gain the approval of many Americans.

7. According to the passage, President Kennedy urged Americans to

   (A) take action for peace and justice.
   (B) ask the country for help if they needed it.
   (C) vote for him as president.
   (D) travel to foreign countries and ask for help.

8. In line 14, the word "ascertain" most nearly means

   (A) enforce.
   (B) help.
   (C) mistake.
   (D) understand.

9. The story of Brenda Sue Wesson (lines 51-55) is included to show

   (A) that President Kennedy was able to reach the international community.
   (B) that President Kennedy's speech was demanding and problematic.
   (C) that President Kennedy was even able to win over young children through his speech.
   (D) that President Kennedy's speech was easy to understand.

10. It can be inferred from the fifth paragraph (lines 37-46) that President Kennedy

    (A) tried to win over some people who had not voted for him by giving a great inaugural speech.
    (B) was able to deliver a great political speech without much practice.
    (C) wrote the speech by himself at the breakfast table.
    (D) did not take his new role in office very seriously.

Go on to the next page. ➤

Questions 11-15

When I was first learning to drive, I thought I would get more direction. That is, when I had received my driving permit as a young teen, I thought that my parents would be more detailed about telling me what to do. Instead, they were mostly nervous and upset with me for not being a good driver already.

The first time I took my mom's car for a spin with her at my side, we went for a quick run to the grocery store. We were in for an eye-opening evening. I made a left turn onto an uphill highway ramp, overestimated how much I had to turn the steering wheel, and drove my mother's huge Chevrolet onto the curb for a short distance. I quickly recovered, and all seemed fine, except for the fact that a police officer was right behind me, and he had watched the entire scene. That's right, I got pulled over even before I had completed driving my first mile.

Another time, my dad was in the passenger seat, and I was driving his car on a rather narrow local street. "Why are you driving so close to the other cars?" he demanded, as I whizzed by some parked cars. I thought to myself that I wanted to stay on my side of the street, but I didn't know that doing so didn't make any sense if there were no other cars driving in the opposite direction.

I have since logged hundreds of thousands of miles over decades of driving. However, driving well took more than a few months for me to figure out. Like most things, I had to learn to drive well by experiencing it all by myself.

RC

3

11. The author's main purpose in this passage is to

    (A) explain how to drive well.
    (B) describe a learning experience.
    (C) discuss the dangers of driving with limited experience.
    (D) analyze attitudes toward driving.

12. The word "recovered" in line 16 most nearly means

    (A) overcame a setback.
    (B) healed a wound.
    (C) corrected a course.
    (D) regained ownership.

13. Why do you think the police officer pulled over the narrator?

    (A) The narrator had made a left turn onto the highway ramp.
    (B) The narrator had driven onto the curb.
    (C) The narrator was too young to drive.
    (D) The narrator was driving on the wrong side of the road.

14. Why was the narrator's father upset in the third paragraph (lines 21-30)?

    (A) The narrator was driving on the wrong side of the road.
    (B) The narrator was driving down a narrow local street.
    (C) The narrator was driving at a dangerous speed.
    (D) The narrator was driving unnecessarily close to the parked cars.

15. With which of these statements would the author most likely agree?

    (A) The only way to learn is by making mistakes.
    (B) Driving is hard, and driving well is even harder.
    (C) Experience is the best teacher.
    (D) Direct instruction is the easiest way to learn.

Go on to the next page. ➤

Questions 16-20

Why did plastic become so popular? In order to find out, we have to go back to the beginning. It began with a contest. A New York firm offered $10,000 to a person who could invent an alternative to ivory. The reason was that the game of billiards was becoming popular, and natural ivory was getting harder to acquire.

In 1869, John Wesley Hyatt solved the problem. He treated cellulose, a material that comes from plants, with a white waxy solid called camphor. What resulted was a plastic that could be molded into different shapes and also made to imitate other substances like ivory.

Things moved quickly from there. In 1907, Leo Baekeland invented Bakelite, the first fully synthetic plastic. After this discovery, the world was to be changed forever. Now that people could produce just about anything without being held back by the limited supply of natural resources, plastic started to appear everywhere. Furthermore, as manufacturing ramped up in the U.S. during World War II, plastics came into high demand for military uses, such as plexiglass for fighter planes and nylon for parachutes, rope, and body armor.

Over the last century, plastic has become an enormous part of people's lives. Household, medical, fashion, industrial, military, food, agricultural, educational, technological, and so many other types of items are made of plastic. It is difficult for most people to imagine a single day without the use of something that is made of plastic.

As practical as plastic has been for humans, it is now posing as big of a problem for the earth. A plastic bag takes about 1,000 years to break down. Plastics in the oceans are breaking down into tiny pieces called microplastics and being eaten by fish. Scientists say that microplastic pollution is not only in the ocean but also in soil, tap water, and even in indoor air.

Plastics are important to people and will not disappear from our lives anytime soon. As a result, scientists are finding ways to make plastic more sustainable and even biodegradable. For the foreseeable future, it seems that plastics will continue to be a part of the earth.

RC

3

16. What is the main idea of this passage?

    (A) Plastic was vital to the U.S. war effort during World War II.
    (B) Plastic continues to contribute to pollution levels at an alarming rate.
    (C) Plastic has become incredibly common and has had an immense impact on our world.
    (D) Plastic was invented as an alternative to ivory.

17. According to the passage, Bakelite is

    (A) the first fully synthetic plastic.
    (B) manufactured from plants.
    (C) John Wesley Hyatt's most well-known invention.
    (D) A brand of plastic-based baking pots and pan.

18. The passage provides enough information to answer which question?

    (A) Which company offered $10,000 to John Wesley Hyatt?
    (B) What happens to fish when they eat microplastics?
    (C) During which war did manufacturers start using plastic for military equipment?
    (D) When will people stop using plastic?

19. In line 49, the word "sustainable" most nearly means

    (A) constrainable.
    (B) consumable.
    (C) disposable.
    (D) maintainable.

20. It can be inferred from the last paragraph that

    (A) scientists are close to developing an alternative to plastic.
    (B) plastic reserves are quickly becoming depleted.
    (C) scientists hope to create plastics that are even longer lasting than conventional plastics.
    (D) plastics will continue to be used until an equally viable alternative is found.

Go on to the next page. ➤

Questions 21-25

When Christopher Columbus came from Spain to the New World, he saw some native people cooking meat slowly by using young green wood so that the food and wood would not burn at high temperatures. The Spanish called this method of cooking *barbacoa*, and it spread throughout Mexico. In America, the word for this way of cooking became known as "barbecue."

Barbecue means cooking meat in low heat for a long time over an indirect flame. There are four main regions that boast of particular styles of American barbecue: Memphis, the Carolinas, Kansas City, and Texas.

The first regional style is Memphis, which of course comes from Tennessee. They love pork, and they use a dry rub, not a sauce, to season the meat before cooking. The seasoning includes garlic, paprika, and other ingredients. There is also a thin, tangy tomato-based sauce that will come with your barbecue plate to flavor your pork.

The next regional style comes from the Carolinas, both North and South. They also choose to barbecue pork. The two states cook the pork the same way, but the North uses a vinegar and spice mixture to season the meat, while the South uses a mustard-based sauce that also has vinegar and some brown sugar, too.

In Kansas City, they like to use all kinds of meats, like beef, pork, and lamb. The meat is cooked with a dry rub for a very long time over low heat. After cooking, the barbecue is typically served with a signature barbecue sauce and french fries.

The final regional style of American barbecue comes from Texas, where they mainly use beef and pork. When eating Texas barbecue, you may find sausage, beef brisket, or ribs in a huge pile in front of you.

Other states such as Alabama, Virginia, and even Hawaii have their own styles of barbecue. Barbecue is one of the most popular ways of cooking in the United States. Even though not everyone eats meat, it is clear that, for those who do, barbecue is largely favored by millions of Americans.

RC   3

21. Which sentence best expresses the main idea of this passage?

    (A) Native peoples in the Americas invented barbecue.
    (B) A large number of people love barbecue.
    (C) There are many styles of barbecue.
    (D) Each state in the United States has a different style of barbecue.

22. In line 6, the word "barbacoa" is in italics to

    (A) specify a technical term.
    (B) signify a foreign word within English text.
    (C) add additional emphasis to the word.
    (D) signify a character's unspoken thoughts.

23. It can be inferred from the passage that "green wood" was used for cooking *barbacoa* because

    (A) its green color prevents the flame from getting red hot.
    (B) it does not produce as much smoke as old wood.
    (C) it imparts a unique flavor to the meat.
    (D) its moisture limits the rate and temperature at which it burns.

24. Which regions represent the main styles of barbecue?

    (A) Alabama, Virginia, and Hawaii
    (B) Spain, the New World, and Mexico
    (C) Memphis, the Carolinas, Kansas City, and Texas
    (D) America, Mexico, and Spain

25. According to the passage, barbecue styles differ most in terms of

    (A) sauce base and ingredients.
    (B) cooking temperature and time.
    (C) type and cut of meat.
    (D) accompanying side dishes.

STOP.

Section 4: Mathematics Achievement
30 Questions — 30 Minutes

1. Use the rectangle to answer the question.

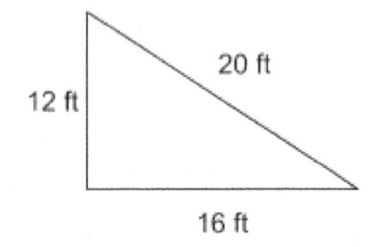

   What is the perimeter of the triangle?
   ($P = s + s + s$)

   (A) 28 feet
   (B) 48 feet
   (C) 96 feet
   (D) 192 feet

2. A total of 32 people were asked which type type of juice (apple, orange, or grape) they preferred to drink with breakfast. If 9 people preferred apple juice, and 15 preferred orange juice, how many children preferred grape juice?

   (A) 5
   (B) 7
   (C) 8
   (D) 11

3. What is the name of a polygon that has five sides?

   (A) quadrilateral
   (B) hexagon
   (C) heptagon
   (D) pentagon

4. What is the standard form for five hundred five thousand thirty-six?

   (A) 500,536
   (B) 505,036
   (C) 553,600
   (D) 505,360

5. Use the number line to answer the question.

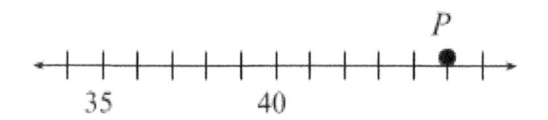

   What number is represented by point P on the number line?

   (A) 44
   (B) 45
   (C) 46
   (D) 47

Go on to the next page. ➤

MA   4

6. An irrigation company manufactures three different diameters of pvc pipe. The pipes were tested to see their water output. The test was run for 4 minutes at a relatively constant water pressure, and the total output was measured at 1 minute intervals. The table shows the collected data.

Water Flow Rate Experiment

Time	½"	¾"	1"
0 min	0 gal	0 gal	0 gal
1 min	14 gal	23 gal	27 gal
2 min	28 gal	47 gal	54 gal
3 min	43 gal	69 gal	81 gal
4 min	57 gal	92 gal	107 gal

At 3 minutes, how many more gallons had the 1" pvc pipe output than the ½" pipe?

(A) 12 gallons
(B) 26 gallons
(C) 38 gallons
(D) 50 gallons

---

7. Which fraction is equivalent to 0.7?

(A) $\frac{1}{7}$
(B) $\frac{7}{10}$
(C) $\frac{1}{70}$
(D) $\frac{7}{100}$

8. What is the value of the expression $2,000 - 365$?

(A) 1,635
(B) 1,645
(C) 1,735
(D) 1,745

9. If $4 \times (\square + 2) = 36$, what number does $\square$ represent?

(A) 3
(B) 4
(C) 5
(D) 7

10. What is the sum of 2.3 and 4.9?

(A) $6\frac{1}{5}$
(B) $7\frac{1}{5}$
(C) $7\frac{2}{5}$
(D) $7\frac{3}{5}$

Go on to the next page. ➤

MA

4

11. The graph shows the average number of flights per day of four airports.

AVERAGE NUMBER OF FLIGHTS PER DAY OF FOUR AIRPORTS

John Wayne	✈ ✈
Los Angeles	✈ ✈ ✈ ✈ ✈ ✈
Ontario	✈ ✈ ✈
San Diego	✈ ✈ ✈ ✈ ✈

✈ = 250 flights

On average, how many more flights per day pass through Los Angeles than John Wayne?

(A) 250
(B) 400
(C) 500
(D) 1,000

12. The Louvre museum has a total gallery area of 72,700 m². Which museum has a gallery area closest to $\frac{1}{3}$ that of the Louvre museum?

(A) The National Gallery of Art, which has an area of 25,200m².
(B) The Tokyo National Museum, which has an area of 38,000m².
(C) The Vatican Museums, which have an area of 43,000m².
(D) The National Museum of China, which has an area of 65,000m².

13. Use the diagram to answer the question.

◨ ☐ ☐ ☐ ◨

☐ ◨ ☐ ◨ ☐

If one of the blocks is picked at random, what is the chance that it will be a ☐?

(A) 1 out of 4
(B) 1 out of 3
(C) 1 out of 2
(D) 2 out of 3

Go on to the next page. ➤

14. Use the table to answer the question.

RACE TIMES IN SECONDS

Race 1	52	65	64	54	62
Race 2	58	69	55	54	52
Race 3	52	64	57	62	64
Race 4	64	58	65	64	62

What is the mode of this set of data?

(A) 52
(B) 54
(C) 64
(D) 65

---

15. Use the set of numbers shown to answer the question.

$$\{ 4, 6, 8, 9, 10, \dots \}$$

Which describes this set of numbers?

(A) prime numbers
(B) composite numbers
(C) even numbers
(D) odd numbers

16. Which fraction is between $\frac{1}{4}$ and $\frac{7}{8}$?

(A) $\frac{3}{4}$
(B) $\frac{1}{5}$
(C) $\frac{1}{8}$
(D) $\frac{9}{10}$

17. Use the number sequence to answer the question.

1, 2, 4, 8, 16, 32, ___

What is the next number in the sequence?

(A) 60
(B) 62
(C) 64
(D) 66

18. Which fraction is equivalent to 0.2?

(A) $\frac{3}{15}$
(B) $\frac{5}{20}$
(C) $\frac{2}{5}$
(D) $\frac{5}{10}$

MA

4

19. Use the histogram to answer the question.

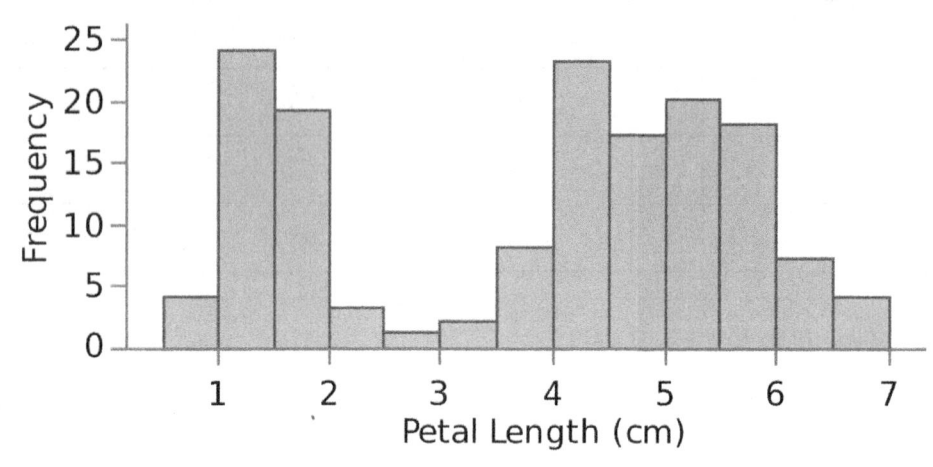

PETAL LENGTH FREQUENCY

Which of the following petal lengths occurred most frequently?

(A) 6cm to 7cm
(B) 5cm to 6cm
(C) 2cm to 3cm
(D) 1cm to 2cm

20. Sean buys five items costing $1.49, $7.99, $0.99, $3.99, and $12.99. What is Sean's estimated total cost?

(A) Between $20 and $25
(B) Between $25 and $30
(C) Between $30 and $35
(D) Between $35 and $40

21. What is the perimeter of a rectangle that has a length of 11 centimeters and a width of 7 centimeters?

(A) 18 centimeters
(B) 34 centimeters
(C) 36 centimeters
(D) 77 centimeters

Go on to the next page. ➤

MA

4

22. Use the coordinate grid to answer the question.

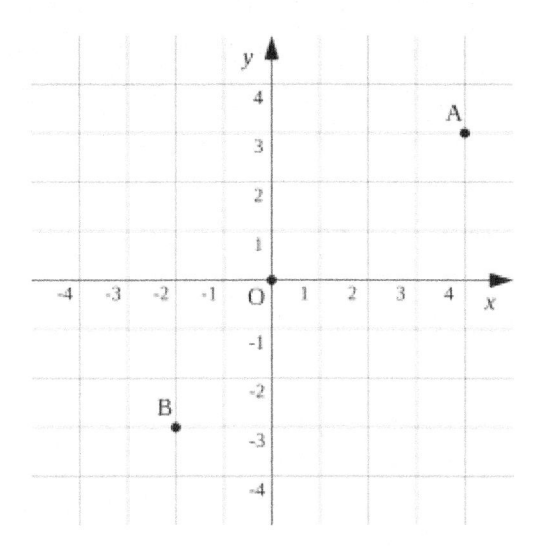

What are the coordinates of point *B* in the figure?

(A) (4, 3)
(B) (3, 4)
(C) (-2, -3)
(D) (-3, -2)

23. Trevor had $7\frac{5}{8}$ feet of rope. He used $5\frac{3}{4}$ feet of the rope as a clothesline. How many feet of rope does he have left?

(A) $1\frac{7}{8}$
(B) $1\frac{1}{2}$
(C) $2\frac{7}{8}$
(D) $2\frac{3}{4}$

24. Which number is divisible by 7 with a remainder of 2?

(A) 28
(B) 29
(C) 30
(D) 31

25. What is the sum of 5.32 and 2.6?

(A) 7.38
(B) 7.92
(C) 8.38
(D) 8.92

26. Use the number sequence to answer the question.

2, 9, 16, ___, 30, 37

What is the missing number in the sequence?

(A) 20
(B) 21
(C) 23
(D) 25

27. What is the standard form for five hundred twenty-six thousand sixty-seven?

(A) 5,267
(B) 52,667
(C) 526,670
(D) 526,067

Go on to the next page. ➤

ISEE LL Test #3: Meri-ISEE LL3

MA

28. What is the value of the expression 394 + 217?

   (A) 511
   (B) 591
   (C) 601
   (D) 611

29. Which expression is equal to 34?

   (A) $8 \times 5 - (4 + 2)$
   (B) $8 \times (5 - 4) + 2$
   (C) $(8 \times 5) - 4 + 2$
   (D) $(8 \times 5 - 4) + 2$

30. If the area of a rectangle is 36 m², which equation can be used to determine the width of the rectangle? ($A = lw$, where A = Area, l = Length, and w = Width.)

   (A) $w = 36 + l$
   (B) $w = 36 - l$
   (C) $w = \frac{36}{l}$
   (D) $w = \frac{l}{36}$

STOP.

BLANK PAGE

E

5

Section 5: Essay
30 Minutes

Directions:

You have 30 minutes to plan and write an essay on the topic printed below. Do not write on another topic.

The essay gives you an opportunity to demonstrate your writing skills. The quality of your writing is much more important than the quantity of your writing. Try to express your thoughts clearly and write enough to communicate your ideas.

Please write or print so that your writing may be read by someone who is not familiar with your handwriting.

You may make notes and plan your essay on this page. However, your final response must be on your answer sheet. You must copy the essay topic onto your answer sheet in the box provided.

Please write only the essay topic and final draft of the essay on your answer sheet.

Essay Topic

> **Outside of your immediate family, who is one of your favorite relatives? Explain why have you chosen this person.**

STOP.

ISEE LOWER LEVEL TEST #4: MERI-ISEE LL4

VR

Section 1: Verbal Reasoning
34 Questions — 20 Minutes
Part One — Synonyms

Directions: Select the word that is most nearly the same in meaning as the word in capital letters.

1. LIMBER:

    (A) alert
    (B) flexible
    (C) indignant
    (D) obstinate

2. NOVEL:

    (A) compatible
    (B) inexperienced
    (C) new
    (D) spirited

3. PALTRY:

    (A) disorganized
    (B) fragile
    (C) simple
    (D) small

4. DETRIMENT:

    (A) allure
    (B) disadvantage
    (C) expense
    (D) novice

5. NONCHALANT:

    (A) benign
    (B) dislocated
    (C) hostile
    (D) unconcerned

6. PERSECUTE:

    (A) accommodate
    (B) elongate
    (C) oppress
    (D) remove

7. VIBRANT:

    (A) amiable
    (B) chaotic
    (C) lively
    (D) shaken

8. HIATUS:

    (A) acquaintance
    (B) fidelity
    (C) gusto
    (D) pause

Go on to the next page. ➤

VR 1

9. GARMENT:

   (A) abyss
   (B) apparel
   (C) flower
   (D) thicket

10. ERRATIC:

    (A) aloof
    (B) sharp
    (C) unpredictable
    (D) wily

11. FRIGID:

    (A) animated
    (B) cold
    (C) contrary
    (D) relaxing

12. VACATE:

    (A) abandon
    (B) adhere
    (C) emulate
    (D) invest

13. BENEVOLENT:

    (A) kindly
    (B) malicious
    (C) sentimental
    (D) somber

14. CONSENT:

    (A) approval
    (B) furnish
    (C) observation
    (D) withhold

15. POVERTY:

    (A) disdain
    (B) neglect
    (C) shortage
    (D) toil

16. REVERT:

    (A) backslide
    (B) confound
    (C) healthy
    (D) insulate

17. CHRONIC:

    (A) abrupt
    (B) bothersome
    (C) continual
    (D) dormant

Go on to the next page. ➤

VR

Part Two — Sentence Completion

Directions: Select the word that best completes the sentence.

18. The Medal of Honor is awarded to armed servicemen who show ------- valor on the battlefield.

    (A) conspicuous
    (B) courteous
    (C) foolhardy
    (D) thoughtful

19. The firemen used helicopters to dump water in a desperate attempt to ------- the flames.

    (A) ferry
    (B) plunder
    (C) quench
    (D) reject

20. With no clear way of achieving victory, the general decided to ------- his forces so that they could fight another day.

    (A) admonish
    (B) mock
    (C) rotate
    (D) withdraw

21. Sometimes soft drink companies ------- consumers by making their products look healthier than they actually are.

    (A) ascend
    (B) deceive
    (C) reclaim
    (D) starve

22. The senator's swift ------- indicated that he was in too much of a hurry to be asked a question.

    (A) frock
    (B) gait
    (C) index
    (D) poise

23. Steven decided to ------- parts from his older car to repair his newer car.

    (A) grapple
    (B) rebuke
    (C) salvage
    (D) sunder

Go on to the next page. ➤

24. Nicholas II, the last emperor of Russia, was forced to ------- the Russian throne in 1917 because of governmental collapse and military defeat.

    (A) compel
    (B) endorse
    (C) relinquish
    (D) strike

25. A(n) ------- beaver can gnaw through three fully-grown aspen trees in an hour.

    (A) aggressive
    (B) evasive
    (C) industrious
    (D) optimistic

26. You would have to be ------- to know how many drops of water are in the ocean.

    (A) apathetic
    (B) flustered
    (C) omniscient
    (D) proficient

27. The climbers each used safety equipment on the mountainside for fear that they might otherwise -------.

    (A) embark
    (B) escape
    (C) foster
    (D) perish

28. Abraham Lincoln was known as the most ------- speaker of his day, and many regard his speeches as the best of any president in history.

    (A) eloquent
    (B) pungent
    (C) radiant
    (D) sullen

29. Tracy was out of chocolate chips, so -------.

    (A) she was also out of flour as well
    (B) she could not make chocolate chip cookies
    (C) she forgot to buy more when she was at the store
    (D) her recipe didn't call for chocolate chips anyway

30. Because the french horn is a difficult instrument to master, -------.

    (A) a few hours of practice can be very rewarding
    (B) it is rare to find one for sale in a music store
    (C) it can produce beautiful music in skilled hands
    (D) many beginners prefer to learn an easier wind instrument first

Go on to the next page. ➤

31. Although class started at seven o'clock sharp, Devin -------.

    (A) always arrived right on time
    (B) was usually several minutes late
    (C) went to bed early the night before
    (D) met with the teacher about his grades

32. Turning your family's food waste into compost helps the environment, and composting -------.

    (A) requires dedication
    (B) is good for the earth's environment
    (C) is pointless if you don't own any plants
    (D) can reduce the cost of planting your garden

33. The past few summers have been very hot, but -------.

    (A) sunscreen is very important
    (B) going to the beach has been a popular pastime
    (C) this upcoming summer should be much cooler
    (D) the past few winters have been unusually warm as well

34. Despite difficulties with her health, Queen Elizabeth II has stated that she -------.

    (A) needs a better team of doctors
    (B) must quickly locate a successor
    (C) will make fewer public appearances
    (D) will not give up her position as queen

QR

Section 2: Quantitative Reasoning
38 Questions — 35 Minutes

1. Which of the following fractions is the largest?

   (A) $\frac{1}{3}$
   (B) $\frac{2}{5}$
   (C) $\frac{3}{10}$
   (D) $\frac{4}{13}$

2. What is the value of x in the equation?
   $\frac{x}{2} - 7 = 11$

   (A) 2
   (B) 8
   (C) 9
   (D) 36

3. A hamburger is twice as expensive as a hotdog, and a hotdog costs one more dollar than french fries. If a hamburger costs six dollars, how much does it cost to order french fries?

   (A) $2
   (B) $4
   (C) $10
   (D) $14

4. How many prime numbers are there between 10 and 20?

   (A) 1
   (B) 2
   (C) 3
   (D) 4

5. Which diagram represents the distributive property?

   (A) $A \times (B + C) = A \times B + A \times C$
   (B) $(A + B) + C = A + (B + C)$
   (C) $A + B + C = C + B + A$
   (D) $A \times B \times C = C \times B \times A$

6. Jerry wants to purchase a new music album online. The album has twelve songs and Jerry can buy the songs individually for $1.19 each, or he can buy the entire album for $10.99. If Jerry wants to buy all of the songs, which expression will show how much money Jerry will save by buying the entire album for $10.99 rather than buying the songs individually for $1.19 each?

   (A) $1.19 \times 12 - 10.99$
   (B) $1.19 \times (12 - 10.99)$
   (C) $10.99 - 12 \times 1.19$
   (D) $10.99 \times 1.19 - 12$

Go on to the next page. ➤

QR   2

7. The triangle below has a base of *B*. Given that the equation for the area of a triangle is *area* = ½ × *base* × *height*, which equation would give the area of the triangle?

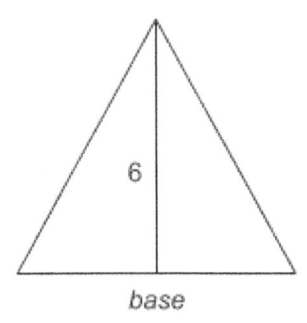

   (triangle with height 6 and base labeled "base")

   (A) area = 6 × *B*
   (B) area = ½ × 6 + *B*
   (C) area = *B* × 6 × ½
   (D) area = 6 ÷ *B* × ½

8. How many units apart are the two points on the number line below?

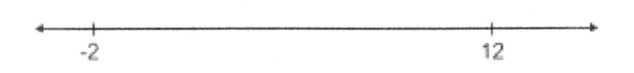

   (number line with points at -2 and 12)

   (A) 2
   (B) 10
   (C) 14
   (D) 24

9. What is the value of *C* in the equation?
   $$24 - 36 \div 3 \times 2 = C$$

   (A) -8
   (B) 0
   (C) 12
   (D) 18

10. What fraction of the shape is shaded?

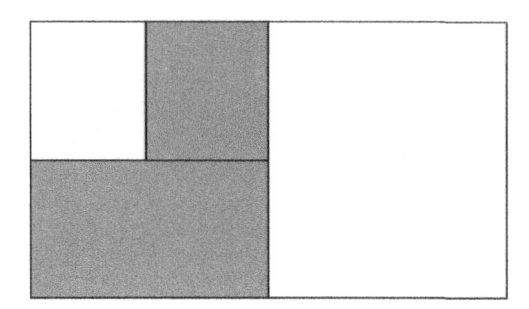

    (A) $\frac{2}{5}$
    (B) $\frac{2}{7}$
    (C) $\frac{3}{8}$
    (D) $\frac{5}{12}$

11. Reyna has to take 2 ½ steps for every 1 step that Matt takes. Reyna walks 240 steps next to Matt, how many steps did Matt make during that time?

    (A) 90
    (B) 96
    (C) 242.5
    (D) 600

12. What is a reasonable estimation for the answer to the problem?
    $$\frac{51 + 147}{102}$$

    (A) between 0 and 5
    (B) between 5 and 10
    (C) between 10 and 15
    (D) between 15 and 20

Go on to the next page. ➤

QR   2

13. The area of the entire figure below is approximately how many times larger than that of the shaded area?

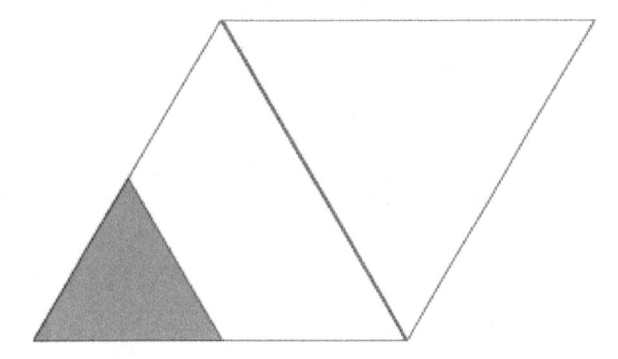

    (A) 4
    (B) 6
    (C) 8
    (D) 10

14. If the base of a triangle is tripled, and the height remains the same, by what factor will the area of the triangle change?

    (A) 2
    (B) 3
    (C) 6
    (D) 9

15. How much larger is the area of a square measuring six feet by six feet than a square measuring five feet by five feet?

    (A) 11 square feet
    (B) 6 square feet
    (C) 4 square feet
    (D) 1 square foot

16. The vertices (-4, 1), (2, 3), (2, 7), (-4, 8) make what type of quadrilateral?

    (A) square
    (B) rectangle
    (C) parallelogram
    (D) trapezoid

17. Soren can walk 2 miles in 30 minutes. If Soren runs twice as fast as he walks, how fast can he run 8 miles?

    (A) 15 minutes
    (B) 60 minutes
    (C) 75 minutes
    (D) 240 minutes

18. There are 24 candies in a box. Half of them are chocolate. Half of those that are not chocolate are caramel. Half of those that are neither chocolate nor caramel are fruit flavored. All of the other candies in the box are black licorice. If a single candy is selected at random from the box, what is the probability of choosing a black licorice candy?

    (A) $\frac{1}{4}$
    (B) $\frac{1}{6}$
    (C) $\frac{1}{8}$
    (D) $\frac{3}{8}$

Go on to the next page. ➤

QR

2

19. If 6 cups of coffee cost $24.00 and 4 muffins cost $12, how much does 1 cup of coffee and 1 muffin cost?

    (A) $7
    (B) $9
    (C) $11
    (D) $12

20. The shaded shape below may be folded along any of the lines shown below.

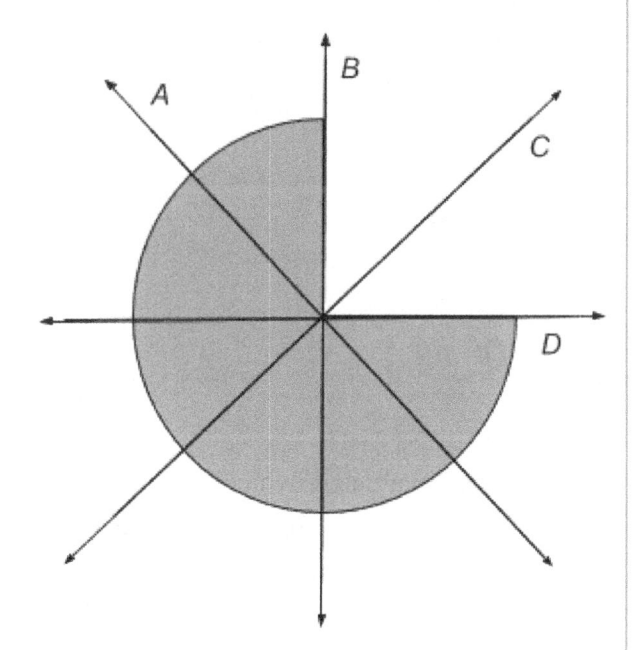

    Which line, when folded, will cause the sides of the shape to overlap exactly?

    (A) line A
    (B) line B
    (C) line C
    (D) line D

21. Which of the following numbers is divisible by 4?

    (A) 124
    (B) 98
    (C) 74
    (D) 50

22. When Kimmery writes a poem for a client, 60% of the money she is paid goes towards running her business. If she was paid $200.00 for her last poem, how much money did not go towards running her business?

    (A) $40
    (B) $80
    (C) $96
    (D) $120

23. Emma's plant is 2 ¼ feet tall, Olivia's plant is 3 ¾ tall, and Cassie's plant is 6 ¾ tall. What is the mean height for the plants?

    (A) 4 ¼ feet
    (B) 4 ½ feet
    (C) 4 ¾ feet
    (D) 12 ¾ feet

24. Which of the following numbers is NOT a factor of 72?

    (A) 9
    (B) 12
    (C) 18
    (D) 21

Go on to the next page. ➤

25. Two trapezoids are shown with their side lengths below.

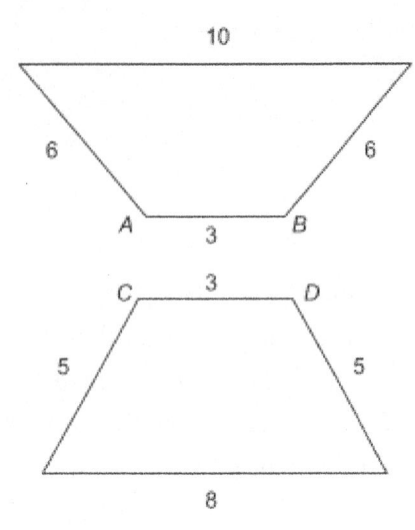

If the trapezoids below were joined along segments AB and CD, what will the perimeter of the resulting six-sided shape?

(A) 40
(B) 43
(C) 46
(D) 50

26. Order the following fractions from least to greatest.

$3\frac{3}{4}, \frac{17}{4}, 3.8, \frac{20}{5}$

(A) $3\frac{3}{4}, 3.8, \frac{17}{4}, \frac{20}{5}$
(B) $3\frac{3}{4}, \frac{17}{4}, 3.8, \frac{20}{5}$
(C) $3.8, \frac{17}{4}, 3\frac{3}{4}, \frac{20}{5}$
(D) $3\frac{3}{4}, 3.8, \frac{20}{5}, \frac{17}{4}$

27. Roland burns 50 calories for every mile that he walks. If Roland burned 2950 calories this week, how many miles did he walk?

(A) 55
(B) 59
(C) 63
(D) 67

28. Nora is putting pencils in boxes. Each box can hold 12 pencils. If Nora has 500 pencils, how many pencils will be left over when she has filled as many boxes as possible?

(A) 0
(B) 4
(C) 8
(D) 10

29. When evaluated, which of the following expressions will have a remainder?

(A) $\frac{60}{8}$
(B) $\frac{52}{13}$
(C) $\frac{42}{3}$
(D) $\frac{35}{5}$

30. Express $9\frac{1}{4}$ as a percent.
(A) 0.0925%
(B) 0.925%
(C) 9.25%
(D) 925%

Go on to the next page.

QR 2

31. Courtney is covering the floor of her bathroom with tiles. If each tile is 3 inches wide and 3 inches long and her bathroom floor is 48 inches wide and 60 inches long, how many tiles will she need?

   (A) 96
   (B) 240
   (C) 320
   (D) 960

32. Ms. Norton divided her class into four teams and sent them to take pictures of as many wildflowers as they could find. The size of the teams and the number of pictures taken per student are shown in the graph below.

	Team Size (in Students)	Number of Pictures Per Student
Team A	4	6
Team B	6	5
Team C	5	4
Team D	7	3

   Based on the information in the graph, which team took the fewest pictures?

   (A) Team A
   (B) Team B
   (C) Team C
   (D) Team D

33. Dalton spent 40% of his money on a new jacket. If Dalton now has 30 dollars, how much did he have before he bought his jacket?

   (A) 20
   (B) 40
   (C) 50
   (D) 60

34. Evaluare the following expression.

   $$\frac{4}{9} - \frac{5}{12}$$

   (A) $\frac{1}{3}$
   (B) $\frac{1}{24}$
   (C) $-\frac{1}{36}$
   (D) $\frac{1}{36}$

35. Which number shows 6 in the hundredths place?

   (A) 39.836
   (B) 41.961
   (C) 64.025
   (D) 72.634

36. Which of the following is the closest to 13?

   (A) 13.1
   (B) 12.91
   (C) 13.01
   (D) 12.9

QR

37. What is the value of x in the equation $x + x + x = 51$?

   (A) 16
   (B) 17
   (C) 18
   (D) 19

38. Ron and Mike are standing 48 feet apart. They then walk toward one another and eventually pass one another. If Ron walked 32 feet and Mike walked 24 feet, how far apart are they now?

   (A) 8 feet
   (B) 12 feet
   (C) 16 feet
   (D) 24 feet

STOP.

RC

Section 3: Reading Comprehension
25 Questions — 25 Minutes

Questions 1-5

1   Cheese is a favorite food for people all
2 over the world and is used to garnish
3 dishes, add incredible flavor, and even
4 catch mice!
5   The story of the invention of cheese is a
6 mystery because, believe it or not, it
7 predates recorded history. That means that
8 cheese was invented so long ago that our
9 history books don't even go back that far
10 into the past! It is estimated, however, that
11 cheese was invented in 8000 BCE when
12 people started to domesticate sheep.
13   Making cheese is a difficult
14 process—you would be ready for a nap
15 after trying to make just one piece of
16 cheese. Professionals who make cheese,
17 called cheesemakers, follow the
18 instructions for making cheese that have
19 been handed down for centuries. First,
20 bacteria is added to milk to create a solid
21 inside the milk called a "curd." The curd is
22 then either aged, cooked, or even covered
23 in mold, depending on the type of cheese
24 the cheesemaker is trying to make.
25   Today, there are over seven hundred
26 types of cheese! Some are soft while others
27 are quite firm. Some are even reported to
28 smell terrible! Cheeses come from
29 countries all over the world, and each takes
30 pride in the cheeses it creates. So whether
31 you are enjoying a pizza with mozzarella (a
32 cheese from Italy), a quesadilla with
33 cheddar (a cheese from England), or a
34 grilled cheese sandwich with Monterey
35 Jack (a cheese from present-day California),
36 you can thank the proud cheesemakers who
37 turn history into something delicious! "Say
38 cheese!"

RC

1. The author discusses all of the following EXCEPT for

   (A) the process for making cheese.
   (B) the history of cheese.
   (C) the most popular type of cheese.
   (D) where certain types of cheese come from.

2. Which of the following could be inferred from the passage about cheesemakers?

   (A) Cheesemakers only make cheeses that their parents have made.
   (B) Cheesemakers in different countries likely make different cheeses.
   (C) Cheesemakers must practice their craft for years to be able to make cheese.
   (D) Cheesemakers are experts at pairing cheeses with other foods.

3. The last sentence of the second paragraph (lines 10-12) implies that

   (A) the first cheese was not made from cows.
   (B) cheese has been around for roughly 8000 years.
   (C) cheese was invented by accident.
   (D) the invention of cheese was widely celebrated at the time.

4. In line 7, the word "predates" most nearly means

   (A) belongs to.
   (B) occurs prior to.
   (C) is included in.
   (D) can't understand.

5. The overall tone of the passage is

   (A) critical.
   (B) informative
   (C) inquisitive.
   (D) sullen.

Go on to the next page. ➤

ISEE LL Test #4: Meri-ISEE LL4

Questions 6-10

"Let's try it out when you get home from school."

Thomas was so excited about his new basketball hoop. He and his dad had bought it online, and it had just arrived in the mail that very morning. The hoop was the kind that had to be attached to a wall or a smooth surface.

Thomas had raced to get ready for school so that he would have enough time to help his dad mount the new hoop right above their garage door. By the time they finished, there was no time left to take out the basketball and try to make it into the new hoop—he had to run or he would miss the bus!

All day at school, Thomas was almost too excited to play basketball with his dad to focus on what the teacher was saying. At 2:30, school let out, and Thomas was soon homeward bound on a bus. It was then that he noticed the dark clouds that loomed overhead. "Oh no," Thomas thought.

Suddenly, it started raining. And not just a little rain, either. It was raining hard! Thomas was very disappointed as he walked home while using his jacket to cover his head from the rain. How could he play basketball now that it was pouring rain?

When he arrived at his house, Thomas saw his dad standing in the driveway. "Get your backpack inside so we can play!" said Thomas' dad.

Thomas was confused. "But it's raining!" responded Thomas.

"I don't mind a little water if you don't!" his dad exclaimed.

Thomas let out a big smile. He didn't mind at all.

RC   3

6. The primary purpose of this passage is to

   (A) explain how to play basketball in the rain.
   (B) criticize Thomas' father.
   (C) describe an experience Thomas had.
   (D) present a potential solution to a type of setback.

7. In line 22, the word "loomed" most nearly means

   (A) assaulted.
   (B) fell.
   (C) hovered.
   (D) observed.

8. It can be inferred that basketball

   (A) takes a long time to play.
   (B) requires a special type of hoop.
   (C) cannot be played in the rain.
   (D) can be played with only two people.

9. Which word best describes Thomas' dad in the passage?

   (A) diligent
   (B) disinterested
   (C) fun
   (D) considerate

10. In the fourth paragraph (lines 17-23), the author implies that Thomas

    (A) got in trouble at school.
    (B) wished he had had time to play basketball before school.
    (C) saw rain on the bus home.
    (D) was excited until he saw the clouds.

Go on to the next page. ➤

RC

Questions 11-15

1   In 1908, Theodore Roosevelt was at the
2 peak of his game. After a landslide election
3 in 1904, Roosevelt continued his presidency
4 as the twenty-sixth president of the United
5 States. Four years later, he had protected
6 national monuments, opened fifty wildlife
7 refuges, created five new national parks, and
8 negotiated peaceful terms between factory
9 and coal mine workers and their employers.
10 If Roosevelt wanted to run for president
11 again, there was only one thing stopping
12 him—himself.
13   Up to that point, no president had served
14 more than two terms in office. Roosevelt
15 had already served two—starting in 1901
16 when President McKinley was assassinated.
17 From that point forward, Roosevelt, who
18 was the vice-president, assumed the
19 presidency.
20   The choice was Roosevelt's as to
21 whether or not he would run for a third term
22 in the White House. Ultimately, he was
23 unwilling to break the two-term tradition
24 and decided not to run. The United States
25 presidency then went to William Howard
26 Taft, whom Roosevelt had endorsed in his
27 place.
28   Taft's presidency brought many changes
29 to the nation that Roosevelt had lead only
30 years before. By changing laws regarding
31 taxing the American people, speaking out
32 against adopting Arizona as the newest state
33 in the United States, and protecting large
34 money trusts, Taft had lost the support of
35 many who had previously endorsed his
36 presidency. Included among those was
37 Roosevelt himself.
38   In 1912, the election for presidency
39 began again, and Taft ran once more for
40 office. This time however, Roosevelt would
41 not support his successor. Instead, he ran
42 against him! Roosevelt created his own
43 political party, called the Bull Moose Party,
44 to run against Taft, who was endorsed by the
45 Republican Party. The people's love for
46 Roosevelt burned bright, and Roosevelt
47 received far more votes than Taft. It looked
48 like the presidency might once again belong
49 to Roosevelt, but the Democratic Party
50 candidate Woodrow Wilson took advantage
51 of the divided Republican Party and won the
52 election. It would be Wilson, and not
53 Roosevelt, who would see the nation
54 through new frontiers, challenges, and,
55 eventually, World War I.

RC

3

11. The primary purpose of this passage is to describe

    (A) the major political issues during Roosevelt's presidency.
    (B) how the Bull Moose Party differed from other parties.
    (C) Roosevelt's choice to run for a third term as president.
    (D) four different presidents and their elections.

12. The function of the fourth paragraph (lines 28-37) is to

    (A) show what caused Roosevelt to change his opinion of Taft.
    (B) compare Taft's achievements to Roosevelt's.
    (C) illustrate the strengths and weaknesses of Taft's presidency.
    (D) describe how Arizona became a state.

13. What does the author imply about William Howard Taft?
    (A) He wanted Woodrow Wilson to win the 1912 election.
    (B) His election for the presidency was influenced by Roosevelt.
    (C) He lost the support of every person who had originally liked him.
    (D) He never ran for president again after losing to Roosevelt and Wilson.

14. As used in line 51, the word "divided" implies that the Republican Party

    (A) was shrinking.
    (B) had turned into the Bull Moose Party.
    (C) disagreed with the Democratic Party.
    (D) had its votes split between multiple candidates.

15. Which of the following questions could NOT be answered with information from the passage?

    (A) Why did the Republican Party endorse Taft in the 1912 election?
    (B) How did Woodrow Wilson win the 1912 election?
    (C) Why didn't Roosevelt run for president in the 1908 election?
    (D) Which political party supported Roosevelt?

Go on to the next page. ▶

Questions 16-20

Few things bring back childhood memories like treehouses. Some children grow up around treehouses—either they or a friend has one in their backyard—and others don't. Unfortunately, the number of children who grow up with treehouses seems to be in decline.

Why are there fewer treehouses than there used to be? Part of the answer is that children today tend to spend less time outside than those of previous generations. Sadly, the treehouse's invitation to adventure and imagination has been taken over by technology such as the iPad.

While treehouses are in decline, there are some who love them enough to make them a way of life. Today, there are restaurants, bedrooms, and even hotels that are treehouses. There is also a TV show called *Treehouse Masters* that showcases the design and construction of huge, impressive treehouses.

For the especially dedicated lover of treehouses, there are treehouse communities, such as Finca Bellavista, located in the rainforests of Costa Rica, where people can build their homes in the trees to live eco-friendly lifestyles away from the technology and busyness of normal life. They build bridges too so they don't have to climb up and down trees to visit their neighbors!

Some treehouses can get pretty huge. The largest treehouse in the world is located in Crossville, Tennessee, and is over fourteen thousand square feet, which is fifteen times the size of the average apartment! According to its owner and builder, Horace Burgess, it took over 11 years to complete. When it comes to treehouses, the only limit is your imagination—and maybe how strong your tree is!

RC

3

16. The main idea of the passage is best expressed by which statement?

    (A) The author fondly remembers his experiences with treehouses.
    (B) Nearly all treehouses are disappearing.
    (C) Despite their decline, treehouses remain popular for many uses.
    (D) The biggest treehouse in the world is in Tennessee.

17. The tone of the passage can be best described as

    (A) cautious.
    (B) disinterested.
    (C) excited.
    (D) thoughtful.

18. In line 23, the word "dedicated" is closest in meaning to

    (A) distracted.
    (B) enthusiastic.
    (C) joyful.
    (D) unusual.

19. What does the author imply about treehouses?

    (A) Treehouses are a safe and fun way to spend an afternoon.
    (B) The best hotels in the world are in treehouses.
    (C) Some people choose to live in treehouses instead of regular homes.
    (D) Soon there will be no treehouses left in the world.

20. The last sentence in the second paragraph (lines 12-14) implies that

    (A) people cannot own a treehouse and an iPad at the same time.
    (B) technology has made people less imaginative.
    (C) the author is sad that he or she never got to own a treehouse.
    (D) what children do for fun has been changed by technology.

Go on to the next page. ➤

RC

Questions 21-25

Hockey, figure skating, speed skating, and more—there are so many things you can do with a pair of ice skates. Ice skating is a popular hobby and sport enjoyed by people of all ages. But how did this favorite pastime come about? To many, it seems unlikely that it would have been discovered in the first place—whose idea was it to strap sharp blades to their feet and slide out into the middle of a frozen lake?

Surprisingly, the earliest evidence we have of ice skating is a pair of skates made from animal bones that were found at the bottom of a lake in northern Europe. Experts estimate that the skates are nearly five thousand years old.

Until the 17th century, ice skating was mainly used for transportation across frozen bodies of water. When the English discovered ice skating, which was some time during the reign of King Charles II, it went from merely a means of transportation to a celebrated racing sport, with events featuring hundreds of skaters racing down frozen canals for the title of being the fastest skater around.

However, the evolution of skating as we see it today was still a long way off. It wasn't until 1865 when American skater Jackson Haines invented a new type of skating blade, as well as a piece of metal called a "toe pick," that figure skating was born. Since then, ice skating has made leaps and bounds, making its way into the Olympics in the form of hockey, speed skating, and figure skating. Today, it is a popular pastime for those who have access to an ice skating rink or a frozen body of water.

RC   3

21. This passage was probably written to

    (A) explain the role of King Charles II in the creation of figure skating.
    (B) describe how hockey was invented.
    (C) relate the history of how ice skates were used.
    (D) compare the different types of ice skating.

22. According to the passage, what ice skating sport was most likely invented first?

    (A) speed skating
    (B) hockey
    (C) figure skating
    (D) All three were invented at the same time.

23. Which word best describes Jackson Haines in the passage?

    (A) determined
    (B) wise
    (C) hard-working
    (D) innovative

24. In line 17, the phrase "leaps and bounds" describes

    (A) the technology of ice skating.
    (B) the usefulness of ice skating.
    (C) the popularity of ice skating.
    (D) the fun of ice skating.

25. Which of the following questions could be answered using information from the passage?

    (A) Who was the fastest skater in 17th century England?
    (B) What were the earliest ice skates made from?
    (C) What gave Jackson Haines the idea for the "toe pick"?
    (D) How has ice skating changed in the last few decades?

STOP.

MA

Section 4: Mathematics Achievement
30 Questions — 30 Minutes

1. What is the total area of the shaded region of the following figure?

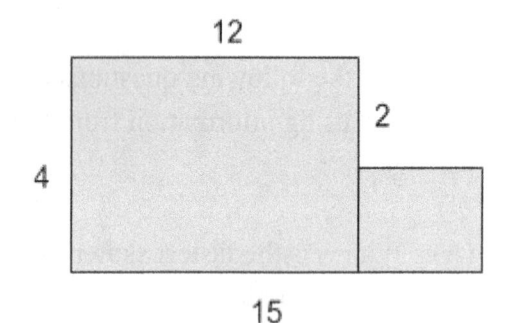

   (A) 45
   (B) 48
   (C) 54
   (D) 60

2. Which of the following statements are true?

   (A) $\frac{17}{8} > 2$
   (B) $\frac{18}{9} > 2$
   (C) $\frac{19}{8} > 3$
   (D) $\frac{27}{9} > 3$

3. Which of the following is equivalent to 0.5?

   (A) $\frac{1}{5}$
   (B) $\frac{10}{5}$
   (C) 5×10
   (D) $\frac{5}{10}$

4. What is the standard form of four hundred forty-seven thousand nine hundred fifty-two?

   (A) 400,952
   (B) 952,447
   (C) 447,952
   (D) 447,259

5. Which expression is equal to 23?

   (A) 40 - 17 x 2
   (B) 27 - 8 / 2
   (C) 17 + 4 x 2
   (D) 18 x 2 / 3

6. If $4 \times \blacksquare - 5 = 39$, then what does $\blacksquare$ represent?

   (A) 10
   (B) 11
   (C) 12
   (D) 13

7. If a field is 45 square feet, what is its area in square yards?

   (A) 5 yards^2
   (B) 15 yards^2
   (C) 135 yards^2
   (D) 405 yards^2

Go on to the next page. ➤

MA   4

8. If Suzie buys clothes costing $2.59, $4.29, $30.79, and $13.29, which of the following is the closest estimation for the total amount she spent?

   (A) $49.50
   (B) $50.00
   (C) $50.50
   (D) $51.00

9. If a car drives at 30 miles per hour, how far can it drive in 90 minutes?

   (A) 3 miles
   (B) 45 miles
   (C) 60 miles
   (D) 90 miles

10. Which of the following statements is true if $x = \frac{4}{5}$?

    (A) $\frac{5}{10} < x < \frac{8}{10}$
    (B) $\frac{14}{20} < x < \frac{18}{20}$
    (C) $\frac{20}{40} < x < \frac{30}{40}$
    (D) $\frac{1}{50} < x < \frac{80}{100}$

11. Use the following sequence to determine the missing term.

    __, 1, 2, 4, 8, 16

    (A) -1
    (B) -½
    (C) 0
    (D) ½

12. Which of the following has a remainder of 1 when divided by 2, and has a remainder of 0 when divided by 3?

    (A) 10
    (B) 12
    (C) 33
    (D) 49

13. The graph shows the number of cars sold on different days of the week.

Day	Number of cars
Monday	X X X X
Tuesday	X X
Wednesday	X X X X X
Friday	X X X
Saturday	X X X X X X X

    How many more cars were sold on Monday than Friday?

    (A) 1
    (B) 2
    (C) 3
    (D) 4

14. Which of the following pairs are multiples of 7

    (A) 49, 147
    (B) 56, 121
    (C) 70, 97
    (D) 84, 101

Go on to the next page. ➤

MA 4

15. If Mr. Burnham is 6.4 ft tall, which of the following is the closest to how tall he is in inches? (1 ft = 12 inches)

    (A) 1/2
    (B) 6
    (C) 70
    (D) 75

16. When surveyed, 9 of the 243 students Southridge Middle School class said that their favorite color is blue. What is the probability that the favorite color of a randomly picked student is blue?

    (A) $\frac{1}{81}$
    (B) $\frac{1}{27}$
    (C) $\frac{1}{9}$
    (D) $\frac{1}{3}$

17. The price of a computer is reduced by 20% and now costs $1000. What was the computer's price before it was reduced?

    (A) $1020
    (B) $1200
    (C) $1,250
    (D) $5,000

18. Which fraction is equal to 0.35?
    (A) $\frac{5}{12}$
    (B) $\frac{7}{12}$
    (C) $\frac{7}{15}$
    (D) $\frac{7}{20}$

19. What is the area of the following shape?

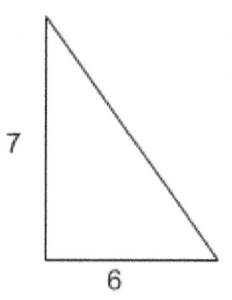

    (A) 13
    (B) 21
    (C) 24
    (D) 42

20. If there are 5 gold bars in a box, and 10 boxes in a crate, how many gold bars are there in 4 crates?

    (A) 125
    (B) 150
    (C) 175
    (D) 200

21. What is the measure of the third angle of a triangle, if the other two are 37°, and 66°?

    (A) 66
    (B) 77
    (C) 88
    (D) 99

Go on to the next page. ➤

MA

4

22. The following figure shows the number of people who prefer a certain type of transportation.

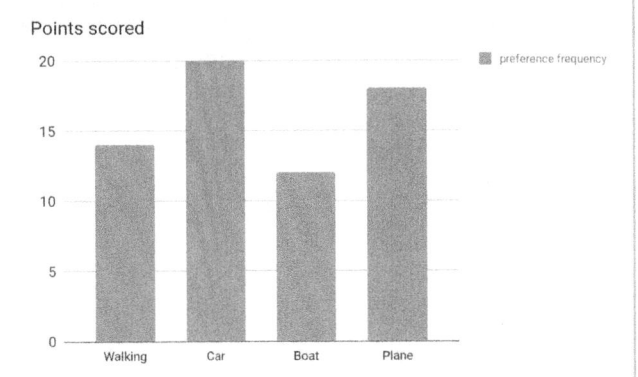

Points scored

[Bar chart showing preference frequency: Walking ~14, Car ~20, Boat ~12, Plane ~18]

According to the histogram above, what type of transportation would a person least prefer if taking a boat is not an option?

(A) walking
(B) car
(C) boat
(D) plane

23. Makenzie and Tanya made a pizza and cut it into slices. Which of the following could be the number of slices they cut the pizza into if the number of slices Makenzie ate is equal to one fourth of the pizza and the number of slices Tanya ate is equal to one third of the pizza?

(A) 6
(B) 7
(C) 12
(D) 18

24. Which of the following is equivalent to $\frac{4}{9} - \frac{5}{12}$?

(A) $\frac{1}{3}$
(B) $\frac{-1}{3}$
(C) $\frac{1}{36}$
(D) $\frac{-1}{36}$

25. Use the number line to answer the question.

[Number line showing 15, A, 60 at equally spaced tick marks]

What number is represented by point A on the number line?

(A) 20
(B) 30
(C) 40
(D) 45

26. Which of the following numbers is NOT a multiple of 1.5?

(A) 4.5
(B) 7.5
(C) 9.5
(D) 12

27. When written as a decimal, the fraction $\frac{3}{11}$ can be most nearly approximated to

(A) Between 0.1 and 0.2
(B) Between 0.2 and 0.3
(C) Between 0.3 and 0.4
(D) Between 0.5 and 0.6

Go on to the next page. ➤

MA   4

28. There are four cups in one quart and four quarts in one gallon. How many cups are in three gallons?

    (A) 24
    (B) 48
    (C) 64
    (D) 120

29. Which of the following points is NOT indicated on the graph?

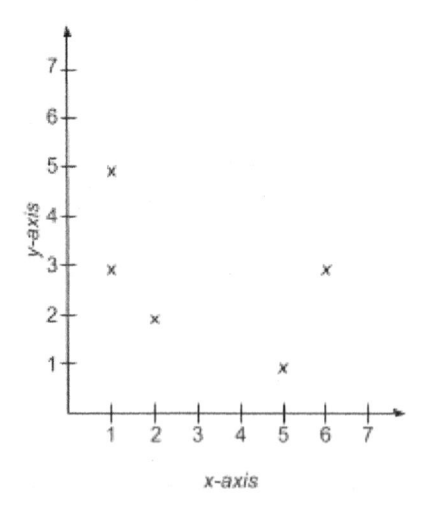

    (A) (3,1)
    (B) (1,3)
    (C) (2,2)
    (D) (5,1)

30. At the deli, Tristan ate three fifths of a sandwich, Kristy ate four sixths of a sandwich, Lucas ate seven tenths of a sandwich, and Andrew ate three fourths of a sandwich. Given that each sandwich was the same size, who ate the most?

    (A) Tristan
    (B) Kristy
    (C) Lucas
    (D) Andrew

STOP.

E

5

Section 5: Essay
30 Minutes

Directions:

You have 30 minutes to plan and write an essay on the topic printed below. Do not write on another topic.

The essay gives you an opportunity to demonstrate your writing skills. The quality of your writing is much more important than the quantity of your writing. Try to express your thoughts clearly and write enough to communicate your ideas.

Please write or print so that your writing may be read by someone who is not familiar with your handwriting.

You may make notes and plan your essay on this page. However, your final response must be on your answer sheet. You must copy the essay topic onto your answer sheet in the box provided.

Please write only the essay topic and final draft of the essay on your answer sheet.

Essay Topic

> **Describe your perfect weekend. What would you do and why?**

STOP.

ISEE LOWER LEVEL TEST #5: MERI-ISEE LL5

Section 1: Verbal Reasoning
34 Questions — 20 Minutes
Part One — Synonyms

Directions: Select the word that is most nearly the same in meaning as the word in capital letters.

1. VALIANT:

    (A) anxious
    (B) brave
    (C) terrified
    (D) timid

2. ABOLISH:

    (A) begin
    (B) create
    (C) end
    (D) retain

3. ELUDE:

    (A) assist
    (B) encounter
    (C) escape
    (D) support

4. ANTAGONIST:

    (A) character
    (B) companion
    (C) enemy
    (D) friend

5. INQUIRE:

    (A) answer
    (B) ask
    (C) certain
    (D) ignore

6. COMPENSATE:

    (A) damage
    (B) forfeit
    (C) penalize
    (D) repay

7. PREDICAMENT:

    (A) advantage
    (B) dilemma
    (C) grief
    (D) solution

8. EXASPERATE:

    (A) delight
    (B) irritate
    (C) pacify
    (D) please

Go on to the next page. ➤

VR

9. RETAIN:

   (A) absorb
   (B) afraid
   (C) forget
   (D) lack

10. DUBIOUS:

    (A) clear
    (B) secure
    (C) serious
    (D) skeptical

11. SCARCE:

    (A) common
    (B) deceive
    (C) frequent
    (D) rare

12. INDUSTRIOUS:

    (A) confident
    (B) daring
    (C) hardworking
    (D) lethargic

13. AROMA:

    (A) nose
    (B) route
    (C) smell
    (D) wander

14. MISCHIEF:

    (A) advantage
    (B) behavior
    (C) boss
    (D) trouble

15. VIVID:

    (A) bright
    (B) dull
    (C) typical
    (D) vague

16. NEGLECT:

    (A) attention
    (B) care
    (C) disregard
    (D) remember

17. CONVERT:

    (A) change
    (B) maintain
    (C) receive
    (D) remain

Go on to the next page. ➤

Part Two — Sentence Completion

Directions: Select the word that best completes the sentence.

18. After discovering how the dodo bird became extinct, the researcher was excited to share her findings with her -------.

    (A) colleague
    (B) narrator
    (C) pedestrian
    (D) protagonist

19. Before Mary could receive the blood transfusion, the doctors had to find a donor with a ------- blood type.

    (A) concise
    (B) compatible
    (C) duplicate
    (D) visible

20. The hotel's ------- were lacking nothing. Each room came with a fully stocked kitchen, giant bed, movie library, and private pool.

    (A) accomodations
    (B) achievements
    (C) documents
    (D) exhibits

21. Rather than screaming insults back at his opponent, George remained calm, ------- replying that it would behoove all participants in the debate to stay on subject.

    (A) happily
    (B) nonchalantly
    (C) unevenly
    (D) unruly

22. Celeste was relieved when she realized that even though she had dropped her laptop running up the stairs, the computer was still -------.

    (A) detectable
    (B) feeble
    (C) functional
    (D) luxurious

23. As Charlie reminisced about her childhood with her grandmother, she began to feel -------.

    (A) senseless
    (B) sentimental
    (C) sluggish
    (D) terrified

Go on to the next page.

24. "------- your coach will get you nowhere," said Ray's father. "If you want to make first string, instead of praising Coach Peterson's NFL career, you need to practice through the entire summer, even on days off."

    (A) Alarming
    (B) Flattering
    (C) Frustrating
    (D) Reassuring

25. The new recruit was stubborn and -------, ignoring the advice of his superiors.

    (A) confident
    (B) diligent
    (C) genuine
    (D) headstrong

26. Because I sought to ------- my parents by changing the grades on my report card, I was grounded for two months.

    (A) deceive
    (B) deprive
    (C) ignore
    (D) repay

27. It is against school policy for any individual to bully or ------- students and staff members.

    (A) admire
    (B) belittle
    (C) reassure
    (D) withdraw

28. The waitress insisted that the lack of attentiveness to the table was not a -------, but an accidental oversight.

    (A) coincidence
    (B) dare
    (C) mishap
    (D) snub

29. Angela called Todd a ------- because he refused to make a charitable donation after lecturing her on the importance of helping others.

    (A) citizen
    (B) criminal
    (C) hypocrite
    (D) victim

30. The ------- student nervously approached the front of the classroom to deliver his speech.

    (A) aggressive
    (B) brave
    (C) timid
    (D) unique

31. Jessica was ------- to discover that she was going to spend her entire summer in Spain. Filled with excitement, she began to pack her suitcase.

    (A) affected
    (B) disappointed
    (C) elated
    (D) troubled

Go on to the next page. ➤

VR

32. After accidentally making a hole in the wall, the new homeowner discovered his house was ------- with termites.

    (A) excavated
    (B) infested
    (C) persecuted
    (D) reinforced

33. Observers stood in ------- as they witnessed Frederic Chopin skillfully play the piano at age six.

    (A) disbelief
    (B) expectation
    (C) ignorance
    (D) jubilation

34. Reaching an elevation of 14,505 feet, Mount Whitney is the highest mountain in California. Every year, thousands of people set off to complete the ------- climb.

    (A) primitive
    (B) tangible
    (C) treacherous
    (D) urban

QR

Section 2: Quantitative Reasoning
38 Questions — 35 Minutes

1. What fraction of the shape below is shaded?

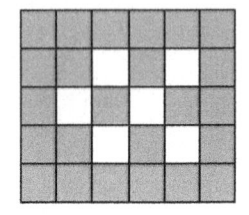

    (A) $\frac{2}{3}$
    (B) $\frac{3}{4}$
    (C) $\frac{4}{5}$
    (D) $\frac{5}{6}$

2. Which of the following is equal to the expression $12 \div 3 \times (3 + 1)$?

    (A) $12 \div \frac{1}{12}$
    (B) $4 \times 3 - 1$
    (C) $\frac{4}{1} \div \frac{1}{4}$
    (D) $3 \times 3 + 1$

3. Which fraction is the largest?

    (A) $\frac{8}{3}$
    (B) $\frac{10}{4}$
    (C) $\frac{14}{5}$
    (D) $\frac{20}{8}$

4. Which story best suits the equation $8 \div \frac{1}{4} = 32$?

    (A) Each student will eat one fourth of a pizza, so eight pizzas will feed thirty-two students.
    (B) There are thirty-two ways that one fourth of eight students can be divided into groups.
    (C) Eight students each ate one fourth of a cake, so thirty-two cakes were eaten in total.
    (D) A class of eight students would need to increase in size by one fourth in order to have thirty-two students.

5. Use the pattern to answer the question.

    BLOOT, LBOOT, LOBOT, LOOBT, ...

    What comes next?

    (A) TOOLB
    (B) LOOBT
    (C) BLOTO
    (D) LOOTB

Go on to the next page. ➤

6. Two swimmers are swimming across rivers of different widths. In the table below, the width of each river is recorded along with the time each swimmer took to swim across the river.

River Width	Swimmer A	Swimmer B
10 yards	14 seconds	16 seconds
15 yards	21 seconds	24 seconds
20 yards	28 seconds	32 seconds
25 yards	35 seconds	40 seconds
30 yards	42 seconds	48 seconds

According to the pattern in this table, approximately how much faster would Swimmer A cross a river with a width of 35 yards than Swimmer B?

(A) 7 seconds
(B) 12 seconds
(C) 49 seconds
(D) 56 seconds

7. Which of the following expresses $\frac{3}{15}$ as a percent?

(A) 3%
(B) 18%
(C) 20%
(D) 35%

8. How many prime numbers are between 30 and 40?

(A) 2
(B) 3
(C) 4
(D) 5

9. Soren and Reggie are wrapping presents. If Reggie can wrap a present in 42 seconds and Soren is three times faster than Reggie, how much time does it take for Soren to wrap a present?

(A) 14 seconds
(B) 21 seconds
(C) 84 seconds
(D) 126 seconds

10. Use the Venn Diagram to answer the question.

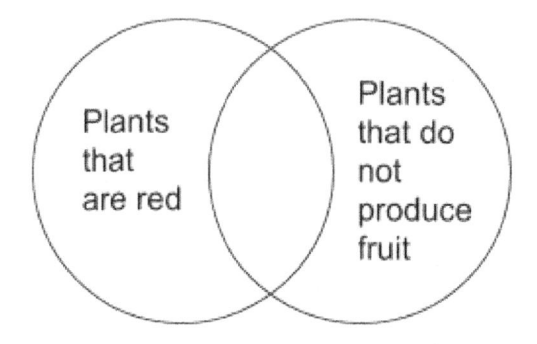

What could be found in the overlapping area of the Venn diagram?

(A) a plant with red fruit
(B) a plant with no red fruit
(C) a red plant without fruit
(D) a fruitless plant without red

Go on to the next page. ➤

11. Given the equations below, what is the sum of a and b?

$$\frac{a}{2} = b$$
$$b + 2 = 8$$

(A) 12
(B) 14
(C) 16
(D) 18

12. Use the table to answer the question.

Input	Output
Σ	Ψ
4	7
6	11
12	23

What is the rule for the function?

(A) $\Sigma \div 2 + 3 = \Psi$
(B) $\Sigma \times 3 - 5 = \Psi$
(C) $\Sigma + 2 \times 3 = \Psi$
(D) $\Sigma \times 2 - 1 = \Psi$

13. Which number has the number 4 in the tenths place?

(A) 1372.46
(B) 1426.17
(C) 1345.63
(D) 1983.04

14. Use the figure below to answer the question.

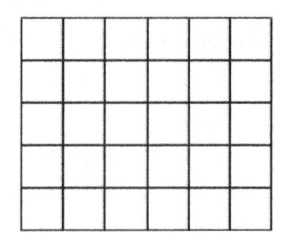

If the length and width of the figure were doubled, what would its new perimeter be?

(A) 22
(B) 30
(C) 44
(D) 60

15. At a grocery store, short-grain rice costs $1.47 per pound. If Roger buys eight pounds of short-grain rice, which of the following is the best estimate for how much money he will spend?

(A) $11.50
(B) $12.00
(C) $13.00
(D) $13.50

16. On a map, three inches represents one mile. If Terry's destination is 18 inches away on the map, how many miles away is Terry's destination?

(A) 6
(B) 9
(C) 12
(D) 18

Go on to the next page. ➤

17. Thirty-five automobiles are parked in a parking lot, and each is either white, red, or blue. There are twice as many white cars as red cars and twice as many red cards as blue cars. How many blue cars are in the parking lot?

    (A) 3
    (B) 4
    (C) 5
    (D) 6

18. Use the figure below to answer the question.

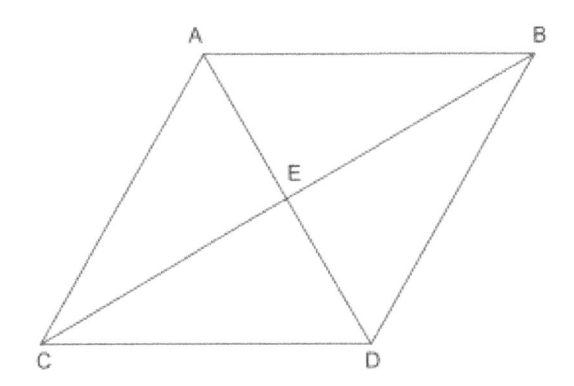

    Daphne wants to use the figure above to draw triangles. She can only trace the straight lines connecting the points A, B, C, D, and E. How many triangles can she draw?

    (A) 5
    (B) 6
    (C) 7
    (D) 8

19. Use the figure below to answer the question.

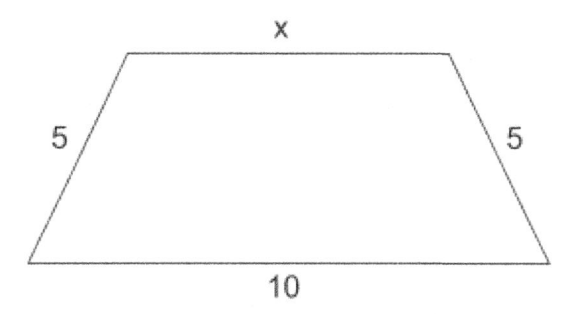

    If the perimeter of the shape is 27, what is the value of x?

    (A) 5
    (B) 6
    (C) 7
    (D) 8

20. If x can be divided by 4 and 7 without leaving a remainder, which number can x also be divided by without leaving a remainder?

    (A) 11
    (B) 12
    (C) 15
    (D) 28

21. The perimeter of an equilateral triangle is $6g$. What is the length of one side of the triangle?

    (A) 2
    (B) $2g$
    (C) 3
    (D) $3g$

Go on to the next page. ➤

QR

22. Use the figure below to answer the question.

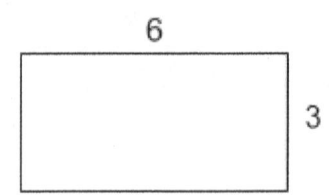

    [Rectangle with length 6 and width 3]

    Which of the following statements about the rectangle above are true?
    ($A = l \times w$ and $P = 2l + 2w$, where A = Area, l = length, and w = width.)

    (A) The area and perimeter are both negative numbers.
    (B) The area is greater than the perimeter.
    (C) The perimeter is greater than the area.
    (D) The area and perimeter are equal.

23. The length of FH is 8 and the length of FG is 3. What is the length of GH?

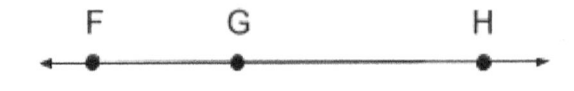

    [Number line with points F, G, H]

    (A) 3
    (B) 5
    (C) 8
    (D) 11

24. Two consecutive numbers have a sum of 17. What is the smaller of the numbers?

    (A) 7
    (B) 8
    (C) 9
    (D) 10

25. Daisy needs an aquarium that holds between 60 and 70 cubic feet of water. Which of the following aquariums, described by their length, width, and height, is the right size?
    ($V = l \times w \times h$, where V = volume, l = length, and w = width, and h = height.)

    (A) 8ft by 3ft by 3ft
    (B) 4ft by 4ft by 4ft
    (C) 5ft by 5ft by 3ft
    (D) 7ft by 4ft by 2ft

26. Which of the following is equal to 120?

    (A) 12^{10}
    (B) $3 \times 4 \times 3 \times 4$
    (C) $(2 + 3) \times (2 + 22)$
    (D) 25×5

27. Use the figure below to answer the question.

    [Number line with points A, B, C, D]

    If AB = 2, BC = 6, and AD = 13, what is the value of CD?

    (A) 5
    (B) 7
    (C) 19
    (D) 21

Go on to the next page.

28. Use the Venn diagram below to answer the question that follows.

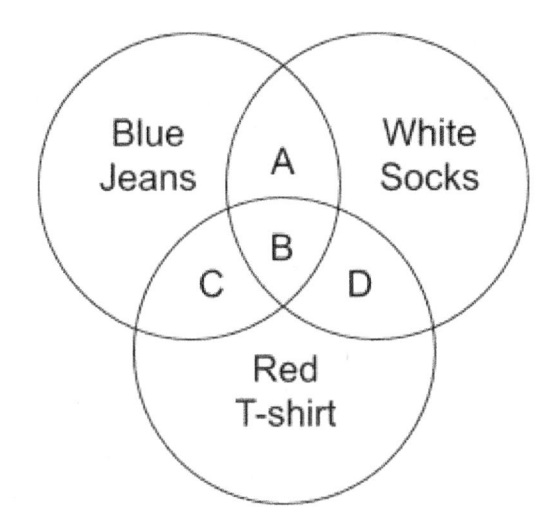

In which region of the diagram would you find Patricia, a 10th grade student who is wearing a red t-shirt and white socks, but is wearing a black skirt instead of blue jeans?

(A) A
(B) B
(C) C
(D) D

29. Which of the following is equal to $\frac{6}{20}$?
(A) $\frac{15}{50}$
(B) $\frac{3}{5}$
(C) $\frac{4}{10}$
(D) $\frac{5}{15}$

30. $62 \div 1000 =$

(A) 6.2
(B) 0.62
(C) 0.062
(D) 0.0062

31. Which of the following shows a line of symmetry?

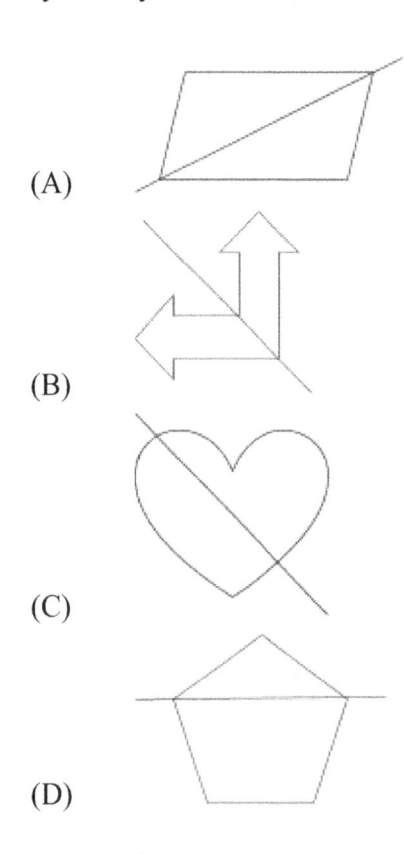

(A)
(B)
(C)
(D)

32. Which of the following is NOT equal to 48?

(A) $2^4 \times 3^1$
(B) $12^2 \div 3^1$
(C) $8^2 - 4^2$
(D) $6^2 + 4^2$

33. $\frac{7}{12} \times \frac{8}{14} = ?$

(A) $\frac{1}{3}$
(B) $\frac{2}{7}$
(C) $\frac{15}{26}$
(D) $\frac{97}{84}$

Go on to the next page.

QR   2

34. Chicago is 1948 miles away from Las Vegas and 1379 miles away from Miami. How much farther is it to Las Vegas than Miami?

   (A) 559
   (B) 569
   (C) 581
   (D) 587

35. Which of the following shows two fifths?

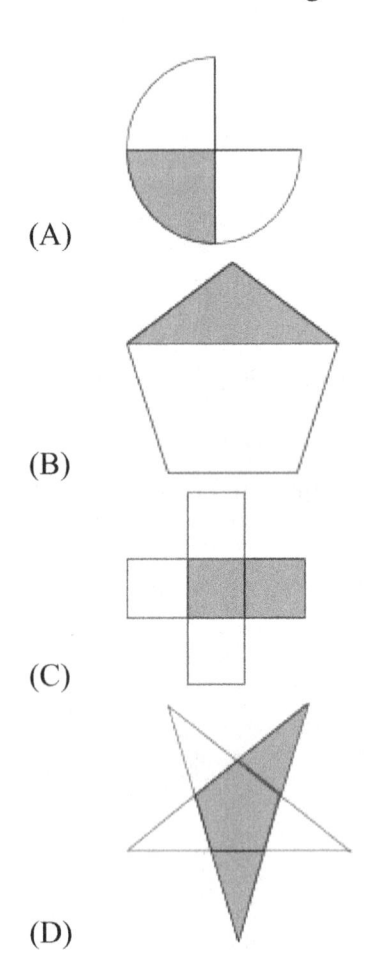

   (A)
   (B)
   (C)
   (D)

36. Which of the following is NOT equal to a whole number?

   (A) $\frac{1}{4} + \frac{3}{4}$
   (B) $\frac{2}{5} + \frac{13}{5}$
   (C) $\frac{3}{3} + \frac{7}{7}$
   (D) $\frac{1}{6} + \frac{6}{1}$

37. On a road trip, Karen drove 840 miles in 14 hours. What was her average speed in miles per hour?

   (A) 48 mph
   (B) 60 mph
   (C) 70 mph
   (D) 72 mph

38. Rob spent 20% of his money on a new pair of jeans. If Rob originally had $200, how much did he spent on his jeans?

   (A) $10
   (B) $20
   (C) $40
   (D) $80

STOP.

Section 3: Reading Comprehension
25 Questions — 25 Minutes

Questions 1-5

1   Gorillas live in groups called troops.
2 Troops tend to be made up of one adult male
3 or "silverback," multiple adult females, and
4 their offspring. However, multiple-male
5 troops also exist. A silverback is typically
6 more than 12 years of age and is named for
7 the distinctive patch of silver hair on his
8 back, which comes with maturity.
9 Silverbacks also have large canine teeth that
10 also come with maturity.
11   Both males and females tend to
12 emigrate from their natal groups. Mature
13 males also tend to leave their groups and
14 establish their own troops by attracting
15 emigrating females. However, male
16 mountain gorillas sometimes stay in their
17 natal troops and become subordinate to the
18 silverback. If the silverback dies, these
19 males may be able to become dominant or
20 mate with the females. In a single male
21 group, when the silverback dies, the females
22 and their offspring disperse and find a new
23 troop. Without a silverback to protect them,
24 the infants will likely fall victim to
25 infanticide. Joining a new group is likely to
26 be a tactic against this. However, while
27 gorilla troops usually disband after the
28 silverback dies, female gorillas and their
29 offspring have been recorded staying
30 together until a new silverback transfers into
31 the group. This likely serves as protection
32 from leopards.
33   The silverback is the center of the
34 troop's attention, making all the decisions,
35 mediating conflicts, determining the
36 movements of the group, leading the others
37 to feeding sites, and taking responsibility for
38 the safety and well-being of the troop.
39 Younger males subordinate to the
40 silverback, known as blackbacks, may serve
41 as backup protection. Blackbacks are aged
42 between 8 and 12 years and lack the silver
43 back hair. The bond that a silverback has
44 with his females forms the core of gorilla
45 social life. Bonds between them are
46 maintained by grooming and staying close
47 together. Females form strong relationships
48 with males to gain mating opportunities and
49 protection from predators and outside males
50 However, aggressive behaviours between
51 males and females do occur, but rarely lead
52 lead to serious injury. Relationships between
53 females may vary. Maternally related
54 females in a troop tend to be friendly
55 towards each other and associate closely.
56 Otherwise, females have few friendly
57 encounters and commonly act aggressively
58 towards each other.

Wikipedia contributors, "Gorilla," Wikipedia, The Free Encyclopedia, https://en.wikipedia.org/w/index.php?title=Gorilla&oldid=837257484 (accessed April 23, 2018).

Go on to the next page. ➤

RC

1. The primary purpose of the passage is to

   (A) relate the responsibilities of female gorillas in a gorilla troop.
   (B) analyze the reasons some gorillas stay in their natal groups.
   (C) describe the physical characteristics of silverback and blackback gorillas.
   (D) discuss the social structure of gorillas.

2. The passage states that the silverback fills which role in a gorilla troop?

   (A) babysitter
   (B) explorer
   (C) groomer
   (D) leader

3. In line 17, "subordinate" most nearly means

   (A) companions.
   (B) disrespectful.
   (C) inferior.
   (D) leader.

4. According to the passage, how do female gorillas act toward each other?

   (A) They are generally friendly if they have the same mother.
   (B) They are generally aggressive toward others of the same age.
   (C) They are always friendly.
   (D) They are always aggressive.

5. The passage provides information to answer which question?

   (A) What is the average lifespan of a gorilla?
   (B) Which gorilla serves as the leader in a gorilla troop?
   (C) What is the primary food source for gorillas?
   (D) How do gorillas care for their young?

Go on to the next page. ➤

Questions 6-10

A floppy disk, also called a floppy, diskette, or just disk, is a type of disk storage composed of a disk of thin and flexible magnetic storage medium, sealed in a rectangular plastic enclosure lined with fabric that removes dust particles. Floppy disks are read and written by a floppy disk drive.

Floppy disks, initially as 8-inch media and later in 5¼-inch and 3½-inch sizes, were commonly used for data storage and exchange from the mid-1970s into the first years of the 21st century. Floppy disks were used with personal computers to distribute software, transfer data, and create backups. Before hard disks became affordable to the general population, floppy disks were even used to store a computer's operating system.

By 2006, computers were rarely manufactured with installed floppy disk drives; however, 3½-inch floppy disks can be used with an external USB floppy disk drive, but USB drives for 5¼-inch, 8-inch, and non-standard diskettes are rare to non-existent. These formats are usually handled by older equipment.

While floppy disk drives still have some limited uses, especially with legacy industrial computer equipment, they have been superseded by data storage methods with much greater capacity, such as USB flash drives, flash storage cards, portable external hard disk drives, optical discs, ROM cartridges, and storage available through computer networks.

Wikipedia contributors, "Floppy disk," Wikipedia, The Free Encyclopedia, https://en.wikipedia.org/w/index.php?title=Floppy_disk&oldid=837858489 (accessed April 25, 2018).

RC

6. Which best expresses the main idea of the passage?

   (A) Floppy disks are available in several different sizes and dimensions.
   (B) There are a variety of storage options available, including USB flash drives, portable external hard disk drives, and optical discs.
   (C) Floppy disks can be used for many important purposes.
   (D) Floppy drives were once the dominant storage medium but have been replaced by other options.

7. Which best characterizes floppy disks as they are described in the passage?

   (A) essential
   (B) expensive
   (C) obsolete
   (D) practical

8. The author implies that good alternatives to using floppy disks include

   (A) portable storage devices.
   (B) disk drives.
   (C) operating systems.
   (D) the internet.

9. In the fourth paragraph (lines 27-35), the author implies that floppy disk drives have been replaced by alternatives that

   (A) cost less to produce.
   (B) provide increased storage size.
   (C) offer less expensive options to consumers.
   (D) are more energy efficient.

10. The function of the first paragraph (lines 1-8) is to

    (A) provide an interesting introduction to the passage.
    (B) summarize one of the main ideas of the passage.
    (C) introduce the main topic of the passage.
    (D) provide evidence for arguments made later in the passage.

Go on to the next page. ➤

Questions 11-15

On a recent trip to the San Diego Zoo to celebrate my mother's birthday, I witnessed something incredible. We were in the "Urban Jungle" area of the zoo, which includes primarily African wildlife. As we made our way around the loop of exhibits, we saw giraffes, a rhino, a kangaroo, flamingos, a cheetah, and a labrador retriever... Wait! What?!

I did a double take. There was a lab sleeping on a bed of hay in a tiny cave with a cheetah only a few feet away. Why was there a dog in the same enclosure as a cheetah? My mom owns a lab. My brother owns two labs. They are happy, gentle family dogs. Aren't cheetahs dangerous predators?

The lab was peacefully sleeping while the cheetah was calmly wandering around and observing the zoo guests through the fence. I knew there had to be a reasonable explanation, so I looked for the informational plaque that is found in front of most exhibits.

Apparently, the lab and cheetah are part of the "buddy system," a program that has become widely used in zoos across the country. While cheetahs are naturally shy and not confrontational, dogs tend to be curious and friendly. By pairing cheetahs and rescue dogs at an early age, the animals bond and become close companions. The dog keeps the cheetah calm and teaches it how to interact with humans, and the cheetah provides companionship for the dog. They do everything together, except eat. Amazing.

RC

3

11. The passage is primarily concerned with describing

    (A) various programs implemented by a zoo.
    (B) the quality of treatment that animals receive at the zoo.
    (C) a new section of the zoo and some of the exhibits that it includes.
    (D) the author's reaction to something he or she saw during a trip to the zoo.

12. In line 29, "confrontational" most nearly means

    (A) aggressive.
    (B) friendly.
    (C) noisy.
    (D) peaceful.

13. Which can be inferred from the last sentence of the second paragraph (lines 16-17)?

    (A) The author does not know much about cheetahs.
    (B) The author has a fear of cheetahs and other large cats.
    (C) The author is curious after seeing a cheetah and a lab in the same exhibit.
    (D) The author can hear others asking similar questions about the exhibit.

14. The passage supplies information to answer which question?

    (A) Why was there a lab and a cheetah in the same exhibit?
    (B) How many African animals are housed at the zoo?
    (C) What do cheetahs usually to hunt in the wild?
    (D) What was the author's favorite exhibit at the zoo?

15. According to the author, a lab was in the cheetah exhibit because

    (A) a zookeeper made a terrible mistake.
    (B) labs originated from Africa and are closely related to cheetahs.
    (C) zookeepers were using the lab to help corner and capture the cheetah for transfer to a different exhibit.
    (D) the lab and cheetah provide companionship for each other.

Go on to the next page. ➤

RC

Questions 16-20

I never used to be afraid of bees. They harmlessly buzzed from flower to flower, amassing pollen for the colony. I didn't bother them, and they didn't bother me.

I had been stung several times when I was younger. My mom would always carefully scrape the stinger from my skin. She would remind me that you don't want to pinch or pull the stinger because you risk squeezing more venom into your skin. She would then make a paste out of meat tenderizer and apply it to the area around the sting. The meat tenderizer helps to break down the venom so that the effects of the sting are minimized. The sting would be uncomfortable for a few hours, swell, and itch for a few days, but it was no big deal.

When I was older and in college, a bee stung me. I calmly scraped the stinger from my arm and applied meat tenderizer, just like my mom had always done. Again, no big deal. But after a couple of hours had passed, every muscle in my body started to ache, and I began to feel tired. I knew I must have been experiencing a minor allergic reaction, and I planned to get medical help if my condition worsened. After about a day, I was back to normal, except for the large itchy bump on my arm.

I was curious why my reaction to the sting had been so much worse than past stings. After some research online, I learned that reactions to bee stings tend to get worse after each sting. Apparently, I could potentially have a serious reaction to a sting. I have been stung a few times since then, but it has always been in the thick skin on the bottom of my foot. I sometimes wonder what kind of reaction I will have to the next sting that is on my arms or torso. I suppose one day I may find out.

RC

3

16. The main purpose of the passage is to describe

    (A) why bee stings can cause itching and swelling.
    (B) how to treat bee stings.
    (C) how the author came to be afraid of bees.
    (D) where most bee stings tend to occur.

17. The author's attitude toward bee stings is best described as one of

    (A) anger.
    (B) concern.
    (C) curiosity.
    (D) interest.

18. The author applies meat tenderizer to his arm (lines 19-21) in order to

    (A) remove the bee stinger.
    (B) break down the bee venom.
    (C) stop the itching.
    (D) moisturize his dry skin.

19. By saying that he worries about what kind of reaction he will have to the next sting (lines 38-40), the author is suggesting that

    (A) his next sting could be worse than previous stings.
    (B) he has developed an unnatural fear of bees.
    (C) he has taken an interest in studying bee sting reactions.
    (D) he has a difficult time predicting the future.

20. In line 3, "amassing" most nearly means

    (A) collecting.
    (B) consuming.
    (C) locating.
    (D) spreading.

Go on to the next page. ➤

Questions 21-25

The American Civil War was fought in the United States from 1861 to 1865. As a result of the long-standing controversy over slavery, war broke out in April 1861 when Confederate forces attacked Fort Sumter in South Carolina shortly after United States President Abraham Lincoln was inaugurated. The nationalists of the Union proclaimed loyalty to the United States Constitution. They faced the secessionists of the Confederate States, who advocated for states' rights to expand slavery.

Out of the 34 U.S. states in February 1861, seven Southern states individually declared their secession from the United States to form the Confederate States of America, or the South. The Confederacy grew to include eleven states but was never diplomatically recognized by the United States government, nor was it recognized by any foreign country The states that remained loyal to the United States were known as the Union, or the North.

The Union and Confederacy quickly raised volunteer and conscripted armies that fought mostly in the South over four years. The Union finally won the war when General Robert E. Lee surrendered to General Ulysses S. Grant at the Battle of Appomattox Court House, followed by a series of surrenders by Confederate generals throughout the southern states.

Four years of intense combat left 620,000 to 750,000 people dead, more than the number of U.S. military deaths in all other wars combined. Much of the South's infrastructure was destroyed, especially its transportation systems, railroads, mills, and houses. The Confederacy collapsed, slavery was abolished, and 4 million slaves were freed. The Reconstruction Era from 1863 to 1877 followed the war, restoring national unity, strengthening the national government, and granting civil rights to freed slaves throughout the country.

Wikipedia contributors, "American Civil War," Wikipedia, The Free Encyclopedia, https://en.wikipedia.org/w/index.php?title=American_Civil_War&oldid=838103503 (accessed May 2, 2018).

RC 3

21. Which sentence best expresses the main idea of the passage?

   (A) The American Civil War resulted in a large number of states being added to the United States of America.
   (B) The Confederacy was composed of many rural farming states that produced food for the majority of the country.
   (C) The American Civil War involved fighting between the northern and southern states, resulting in heavy casualties, damage to infrastructure, and freedom for slaves.
   (D) The American Civil War resulted in Canada and Mexico becoming separate countries from the United States of America.

22. The passage claims that the American Civil War resulted in

   (A) the loss of civil rights by countless Americans.
   (B) more United States military deaths than all other U.S. wars combined.
   (C) a small group of states taking control of the United States government.
   (D) the adoption of the U.S. Constitution by the United States of America.

23. In line 11, the word "advocated" most nearly means

   (A) despised.
   (B) discussed.
   (C) invented.
   (D) supported.

24. In line 15, the word "secession" most nearly means

   (A) disagreement.
   (B) escape.
   (C) vacation.
   (D) withdrawal.

25. According to the passage, what was the main reason that the Confederate States seceded from the United States?

   (A) The United States had been unfairly taxing the Confederate States.
   (B) The Confederate States wanted to be diplomatically recognized by foreign governments.
   (C) The Confederate states wanted to maintain the right of states to expand slavery.
   (D) The Confederate States believed that having 11 states required that a new country be formed.

STOP.

MA

Section 4: Mathematics Achievement
30 Questions — 30 Minutes

1. If $6 + \Gamma \times 3 = 27$, what must be the value of Γ?

    (A) 3
    (B) 7
    (C) 63
    (D) 75

2. At a grocery store, mangoes cost $1.09 each, kiwis cost $0.37 each, and bananas cost $0.26 each. Which of the following is the closest estimation for how much it will cost to buy two mangoes, four kiwis, and one banana?

    (A) $2.00
    (B) $3.75
    (C) $4.00
    (D) $4.25

3. What is the standard form of one hundred sixty-eight thousand, nine hundred six?

    (A) 168,906
    (B) 168,960
    (C) 186,609
    (D) 186,960

4. Which of the following is equivalent to 2.6?

    (A) $\frac{13}{5}$
    (B) $\frac{18}{7}$
    (C) $\frac{10}{4}$
    (D) $\frac{16}{6}$

5. Which of the following statements is false?

    (A) $\frac{1}{2} > 0.4$
    (B) $\frac{2}{3} > 0.6$
    (C) $\frac{3}{4} > 0.7$
    (D) $\frac{4}{5} > 0.8$

6. What is the area of the shaded entire shaded region?

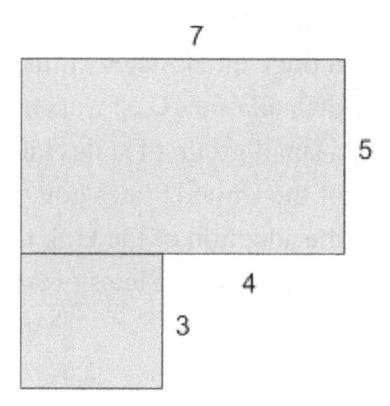

    (A) 44
    (B) 45
    (C) 63
    (D) 95

Go on to the next page. ➤

MA

4

7. Which expression is equivalent to 51?

   (A) $102 \div 3$
   (B) $17 \div \frac{1}{3}$
   (C) $\frac{7}{2} \times 14$
   (D) $13 \times \frac{12}{3}$

8. Charlie hikes at a pace of four miles per hour. How far can she hike in 150 minutes?

   (A) 4
   (B) 6
   (C) 8
   (D) 10

9. Use the following sequence to determine the missing number.

   11, 13.5, 16, 18.5, ___, 23.5

   (A) 20
   (B) 20.5
   (C) 21
   (D) 21.5

10. If twenty beans fit inside one bag and seven bags fit in one box, how many beans are in two boxes?

    (A) 70
    (B) 140
    (C) 210
    (D) 280

11. What is the area of the following shape?

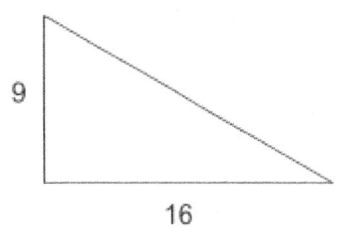

    (A) 25
    (B) 72
    (C) 96
    (D) 144

12. Which of the following is equivalent to $\frac{2}{5} + \frac{5}{2}$?

    (A) $\frac{29}{10}$
    (B) $\frac{29}{5}$
    (C) $\frac{26}{5}$
    (D) $\frac{26}{10}$

13. Use the number line to answer the question.

    What number is represented by point F on the number line?

    (A) 8
    (B) 9
    (C) 10
    (D) 12

Go on to the next page. ➤

14. Which of the following points is NOT indicated on the graph below?

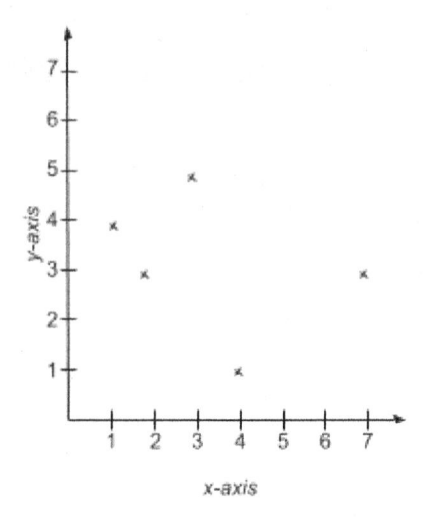

(A) (4,1)
(B) (3,5)
(C) (7,3)
(D) (1,3)

15. One cup is equal to sixteen tablespoons. One cup is also equal to eight fluid ounces. How many tablespoons are equal to two fluid ounces?

(A) 2
(B) 4
(C) 8
(D) 16

16. When written as a decimal, the fraction $\frac{4}{9}$ can be most nearly approximated to

(A) between 0.2 and 0.3
(B) between 0.3 and 0.4
(C) between 0.4 and 0.5
(D) between 0.5 and 0.6

17. Which of the following numbers is NOT a multiple of 3.5?

(A) 7
(B) 10.5
(C) 19.5
(D) 42

18. What is the perimeter of the entire shaded region below?

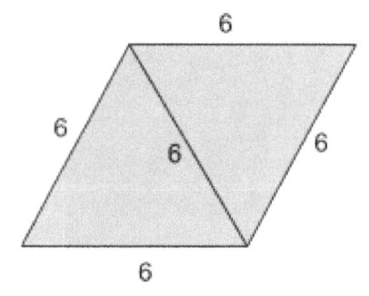

(A) 24
(B) 30
(C) 36
(D) 48

19. On any given day, two out of every five beverages ordered at a local coffee shop are lattes. If on a certain day the coffee shop made six hundred drinks, how many of those drinks were lattes?

(A) 120
(B) 180
(C) 240
(D) 360

MA 4

20. What is the value of the expression
    206.01 + 106.1 ?

    (A) 222.11
    (B) 222.2
    (C) 312.11
    (D) 312.2

21. Danny is dissolving sugar cubes in water and measuring how many seconds it takes each cube to dissolve. He dissolves sugar cubes one at a time at each temperature, and his results are recorded in the graph below. Times for the first, second, and third sugar cubes are recorded in seconds.

Temperature	First	Second	Third
170°	19	20	18
180°	17	17	18
190°	15	16	14
200°	14	12	11

    Based on the information above, at which temperature did the recorded times required to dissolve a sugar cube vary the greatest?

    (A) 170°
    (B) 180°
    (C) 190°
    (D) 200°

22. Which of the following is closest in value to 16.304?

    (A) 16.29
    (B) 16.31
    (C) 16.34
    (D) 16.4

23. Which number is divisible by 8 with a remainder of 3?

    (A) 27
    (B) 30
    (C) 34
    (D) 38

24. What fraction is equivalent to 0.15?

    (A) $\frac{15}{1}$
    (B) $\frac{15}{10}$
    (C) $\frac{15}{100}$
    (D) $\frac{15}{1000}$

25. Tanya wants to fence off a rectangular space of approximately 2500 square feet. Which of the following would create a fenced space closest to the size Tanya wants?

    (A) a fenced rectangular lot with a width of 12 feet and a length of 2 feet
    (B) a fenced rectangular lot with a width of 30 feet and a length of 80 feet
    (C) a fenced rectangular lot with a width of 400 feet and a length of 600 feet
    (D) a fenced rectangular lot with a width of 2000 feet and a length of 400 feet

Go on to the next page. ➤

MA   4

26. Which of the following units of measurement would be most appropriate to measure the amount of oil a baking factory uses in a day?

   (A) inches
   (B) pounds
   (C) gallons
   (D) degrees Fahrenheit

27. What is the name of the quadrilateral shown below?

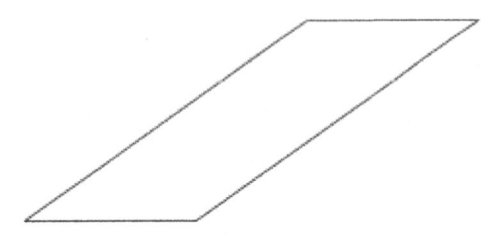

   (A) rectangle
   (B) parallelogram
   (C) trapezoid
   (D) kite

28. Which of the following is equal to $\frac{3}{50}$?

   (A) 0.3
   (B) 0.03
   (C) 0.6
   (D) 0.06

29. Cheetahs are the fastest land animal in the world, capable of running up to 75 miles per hour (mph). Which animal has a maximum running speed closest to $\frac{2}{5}$ that of the cheetah?

   (A) the cow, which can run at a speed of 25 mph
   (B) the kangaroo, which can hop at a speed of 30 mph
   (C) the hyena, which can run at a speed of 40 mph
   (D) the wildebeest, which can run at a speed of 50 mph

30. The number 43 is

   (A) odd and even.
   (B) even and prime.
   (C) odd and composite.
   (D) odd and prime.

STOP.

E

5

Section 5: Essay
30 Minutes

Directions:

You have 30 minutes to plan and write an essay on the topic printed below. Do not write on another topic.

The essay gives you an opportunity to demonstrate your writing skills. The quality of your writing is much more important than the quantity of your writing. Try to express your thoughts clearly and write enough to communicate your ideas.

Please write or print so that your writing may be read by someone who is not familiar with your handwriting.

You may make notes and plan your essay on this page. However, your final response must be on your answer sheet. You must copy the essay topic onto your answer sheet in the box provided.

Please write only the essay topic and final draft of the essay on your answer sheet.

Essay Topic

> **What is your favorite thing to do when you have free time? Explain why this is important to you.**

STOP.

TEST ANSWER KEYS

ISEE LOWER LEVEL TESTS: ANSWER KEYS

ISEE LL Test #1: Meri-ISEE LL1
Answer Key

Verbal Reasoning
1. B
2. D
3. A
4. A
5. B
6. C
7. C
8. C
9. A
10. C
11. A
12. B
13. A
14. A
15. D
16. D
17. B
18. A
19. B
20. B
21. D
22. B
23. A
24. A
25. D
26. D
27. B
28. A
29. A
30. B
31. D
32. D
33. B
34. D

Quantitative Reasoning
1. D
2. C
3. B
4. D
5. A
6. B
7. C
8. D
9. B
10. D
11. D
12. A
13. B
14. B
15. D
16. C
17. A
18. C
19. A
20. B
21. D
22. B
23. C
24. C
25. A
26. C
27. A
28. D
29. B
30. B
31. C
32. D
33. D
34. D
35. C
36. A
37. A
38. A

Reading Comprehension
1. C
2. D
3. C
4. C
5. D
6. A
7. A
8. D
9. D
10. B
11. C
12. B
13. D
14. A
15. D
16. B
17. A
18. C
19. D
20. C
21. B
22. D
23. C
24. B
25. B

ISEE LL Test #1: Meri-ISEE LL1
Answer Key

Mathematics Achievement

1. B
2. B
3. D
4. C
5. C
6. A
7. B
8. C
9. B
10. A
11. C
12. D
13. C
14. D
15. B
16. C
17. B
18. B
19. B
20. A
21. A
22. D
23. C
24. C
25. A
26. A
27. D
28. B
29. A
30. D

ISEE LL Test #2: Meri-ISEE LL2
Answer Key

Verbal Reasoning	Quantitative Reasoning	Reading Comprehension
1. C	1. C	1. C
2. C	2. B	2. C
3. C	3. A	3. B
4. B	4. B	4. C
5. A	5. B	5. C
6. C	6. D	6. A
7. C	7. A	7. D
8. C	8. B	8. B
9. C	9. D	9. A
10. A	10. C	10. C
11. B	11. B	11. D
12. C	12. A	12. B
13. A	13. B	13. B
14. D	14. B	14. D
15. C	15. D	15. A
16. A	16. A	16. D
17. D	17. C	17. C
18. D	18. D	18. B
19. A	19. B	19. A
20. A	20. B	20. B
21. D	21. D	21. C
22. D	22. B	22. D
23. C	23. A	23. C
24. C	24. A	24. A
25. B	25. D	25. B
26. D	26. A	
27. A	27. C	
28. D	28. B	
29. B	29. B	
30. C	30. C	
31. C	31. D	
32. C	32. A	
33. D	33. A	
34. D	34. D	
	35. C	
	36. A	
	37. D	
	38. B	

TEST ANSWER KEYS

ISEE LL Test #2: Meri-ISEE LL2
Answer Key

Mathematics Achievement
1. C
2. B
3. A
4. D
5. A
6. D
7. B
8. A
9. D
10. D
11. A
12. C
13. B
14. C
15. A
16. A
17. A
18. B
19. C
20. C
21. B
22. C
23. C
24. C
25. A
26. C
27. B
28. D
29. D
30. C

ISEE LL Test #3: Meri-ISEE LL3
Answer Key

Verbal Reasoning	Quantitative Reasoning	Reading Comprehension
1. C	1. A	1. B
2. B	2. D	2. B
3. D	3. C	3. B
4. D	4. B	4. C
5. B	5. C	5. C
6. D	6. C	6. D
7. C	7. A	7. A
8. B	8. C	8. D
9. C	9. A	9. C
10. C	10. B	10. A
11. D	11. B	11. B
12. D	12. C	12. C
13. C	13. B	13. B
14. D	14. B	14. D
15. A	15. D	15. C
16. A	16. B	16. C
17. B	17. C	17. A
18. C	18. C	18. C
19. D	19. A	19. D
20. A	20. D	20. D
21. D	21. C	21. C
22. B	22. C	22. B
23. A	23. C	23. D
24. A	24. A	24. C
25. D	25. B	25. A
26. D	26. C	
27. B	27. B	
28. A	28. C	
29. B	29. D	
30. A	30. C	
31. B	31. B	
32. B	32. A	
33. D	33. D	
34. A	34. A	
	35. D	
	36. A	
	37. A	
	38. D	

TEST ANSWER KEYS

ISEE LL Test #3: Meri-ISEE LL3
Answer Key

Mathematics Achievement
1. B
2. C
3. D
4. B
5. B
6. C
7. B
8. A
9. D
10. B
11. D
12. A
13. D
14. C
15. B
16. A
17. C
18. A
19. D
20. B
21. C
22. C
23. A
24. C
25. B
26. C
27. D
28. D
29. A
30. C

ISEE LL Test #4: Meri-ISEE LL4
Answer Key

Verbal Reasoning
1. B
2. C
3. D
4. B
5. D
6. C
7. C
8. D
9. B
10. C
11. B
12. A
13. A
14. A
15. C
16. A
17. C
18. A
19. C
20. D
21. B
22. B
23. C
24. C
25. C
26. C
27. D
28. A
29. B
30. D
31. B
32. D
33. C
34. D

Quantitative Reasoning
1. B
2. D
3. A
4. D
5. A
6. A
7. C
8. C
9. B
10. C
11. B
12. A
13. C
14. B
15. A
16. D
17. B
18. C
19. A
20. C
21. A
22. D
23. A
24. D
25. A
26. D
27. B
28. C
29. A
30. D
31. C
32. C
33. C
34. D
35. B
36. C
37. B
38. A

Reading Comprehension
1. C
2. B
3. A
4. B
5. B
6. C
7. C
8. B
9. C
10. D
11. C
12. A
13. B
14. D
15. A
16. C
17. C
18. B
19. C
20. D
21. C
22. A
23. D
24. C
25. B

TEST ANSWER KEYS

ISEE LL Test #4: Meri-ISEE LL4
Answer Key

Mathematics Achievement
1. C
2. A
3. D
4. C
5. B
6. B
7. A
8. D
9. B
10. B
11. D
12. C
13. A
14. A
15. D
16. B
17. C
18. D
19. B
20. D
21. B
22. A
23. C
24. C
25. B
26. C
27. B
28. B
29. A
30. D

ISEE LL Test #5: Meri-ISEE LL5
Answer Key

Verbal Reasoning	Quantitative Reasoning	Reading Comprehension
1. B	1. C	1. D
2. C	2. C	2. D
3. C	3. C	3. C
4. C	4. A	4. A
5. B	5. D	5. B
6. D	6. A	6. D
7. B	7. C	7. C
8. B	8. A	8. A
9. A	9. A	9. B
10. D	10. C	10. C
11. D	11. D	11. D
12. C	12. D	12. A
13. C	13. A	13. C
14. D	14. C	14. A
15. A	15. B	15. D
16. C	16. A	16. C
17. A	17. C	17. B
18. A	18. D	18. B
19. B	19. C	19. A
20. A	20. D	20. A
21. B	21. B	21. C
22. C	22. D	22. B
23. B	23. B	23. D
24. B	24. B	24. D
25. D	25. B	25. C
26. A	26. C	
27. B	27. A	
28. D	28. D	
29. C	29. A	
30. C	30. C	
31. C	31. B	
32. B	32. D	
33. A	33. A	
34. C	34. B	
	35. C	
	36. D	
	37. B	
	38. C	

TEST ANSWER KEYS

ISEE LL Test #5: Meri-ISEE LL5
Answer Key

Mathematics Achievement
1. B
2. C
3. A
4. A
5. D
6. A
7. B
8. D
9. C
10. D
11. B
12. A
13. D
14. D
15. B
16. C
17. C
18. A
19. C
20. C
21. D
22. B
23. A
24. C
25. B
26. C
27. B
28. D
29. B
30. D

TEST ANSWER KEYS

ISEE Lower Level Test Scale

Raw Score	Verbal Reasoning Scaled Score (760–940) / Percentile Rank (1–99) / Stanine (1–9)	Quantitative Reasoning Scaled Score (760–940) / Percentile Rank (1–99) / Stanine (1–9)	Reading Comprehension Scaled Score (760–940) / Percentile Rank (1–99) / Stanine (1–9)	Mathematics Achievement Scaled Score (760–940) / Percentile Rank (1–99) / Stanine (1–9)
0	774–804 / 1–3 / 1	758–788 / 1–3 / 1	760–792 / 1–3 / 1	760–790 / 1–3 / 1
1	778–808 / 1–3 / 1	762–792 / 1–3 / 1	766–796 / 1–3 / 1	765–795 / 1–3 / 1
2	782–812 / 4–10 / 2	766–796 / 1–3 / 1	772–802 / 4–10 / 2	770–800 / 4–10 / 2
3	786–816 / 4–10 / 2	770–800 / 4–10 / 2	778–808 / 4–10 / 2	775–805 / 4–10 / 2
4	790–820 / 11–22 / 3	774–804 / 4–10 / 2	784–814 / 11–22 / 3	780–810 / 11–22 / 3
5	794–824 / 11–22 / 3	778–808 / 4–10 / 2	790–820 / 11–22 / 3	785–815 / 11–22 / 3
6	798–828 / 11–22 / 3	782–812 / 11–22 / 3	796–826 / 11–22 / 3	790–820 / 11–22 / 3
7	802–832 / 11–22 / 3	786–816 / 11–22 / 3	802–832 / 23–39 / 4	795–825 / 11–22 / 3
8	806–836 / 23–39 / 4	790–820 / 11–22 / 3	808–838 / 23–39 / 4	800–830 / 23–39 / 4
9	810–840 / 23–39 / 4	794–824 / 11–22 / 3	814–844 / 23–39 / 4	805–835 / 23–39 / 4
10	814–844 / 23–39 / 4	798–828 / 23–39 / 4	820–850 / 23–39 / 4	810–840 / 23–39 / 4
11	818–848 / 23–39 / 4	802–832 / 23–39 / 4	826–856 / 40–59 / 5	815–845 / 23–39 / 4
12	822–852 / 23–39 / 4	806–836 / 23–39 / 4	832–862 / 40–59 / 5	820–850 / 23–39 / 4
13	826–856 / 23–39 / 4	810–840 / 23–39 / 4	838–868 / 40–59 / 5	825–855 / 40–59 / 5
14	830–860 / 40–59 / 5	814–844 / 23–39 / 4	844–874 / 40–59 / 5	830–860 / 40–59 / 5
15	834–864 / 40–59 / 5	818–848 / 23–39 / 4	850–880 / 40–59 / 5	835–865 / 40–59 / 5
16	838–868 / 40–59 / 5	822–852 / 40–59 / 5	856–886 / 77–88 / 6	840–870 / 40–59 / 5
17	842–872 / 40–59 / 5	826–856 / 40–59 / 5	862–892 / 77–88 / 6	845–875 / 40–59 / 5
18	846–876 / 40–59 / 5	830–860 / 40–59 / 5	868–898 / 77–88 / 6	850–880 / 40–59 / 5
19	850–880 / 40–59 / 5	834–864 / 40–59 / 5	874–904 / 77–88 / 6	855–885 / 60–76 / 6
20	854–884 / 40–59 / 5	838–868 / 40–59 / 5	880–910 / 89–95 / 7	860–890 / 60–76 / 6
21	858–888 / 60–76 / 6	842–872 / 40–59 / 5	886–916 / 89–95 / 7	865–895 / 60–76 / 6
22	862–892 / 60–76 / 6	846–876 / 40–59 / 5	892–922 / 89–95 / 7	870–900 / 60–76 / 6
23	866–896 / 60–76 / 6	850–880 / 40–59 / 5	898–928 / 96–99 / 8	875–905 / 60–76 / 6
24	870–900 / 60–76 / 6	854–884 / 60–76 / 6	904–934 / 96–99 / 8	880–910 / 77–88 / 7
25	874–904 / 60–76 / 6	858–888 / 60–76 / 6	910–940 / 96–99 / 9	885–915 / 77–88 / 7
26	878–908 / 60–76 / 6	862–892 / 60–76 / 6	–	890–920 / 77–88 / 7
27	882–912 / 77–88 / 7	866–896 / 60–76 / 6	–	895–925 / 77–88 / 7
28	886–916 / 77–88 / 7	870–900 / 60–76 / 6	–	900–930 / 89–95 / 8
29	890–920 / 77–88 / 7	874–904 / 60–76 / 6	–	905–935 / 89–95 / 8
30	894–924 / 77–88 / 7	878–908 / 77–88 / 7	–	910–940 / 96–99 / 9
31	898–928 / 89–95 / 8	882–912 / 77–88 / 7	–	–
32	902–932 / 89–95 / 8	886–916 / 77–88 / 7	–	–
33	906–936 / 89–95 / 8	890–920 / 77–88 / 7	–	–
34	910–940 / 96–99 / 9	894–924 / 89–95 / 8	–	–
35	–	898–928 / 89–95 / 8	–	–
36	–	902–932 / 89–95 / 8	–	–
37	–	906–936 / 96–99 / 9	–	–
38	–	910–940 / 96–99 / 9	–	–

TEST SCALE

Made in the USA
Coppell, TX
27 May 2023